LONGMAN

*h*OMEWORK *h*ANDBO

GCSE

MATHEMATICS

Brian Speed

LONGMAN

HOMEWORK HANDBOOKS

Series editors:

Geoff Black and Stuart Wall

Other titles in this series:
BIOLOGY
CHEMISTRY
GEOGRAPHY
PHYSICS
SCIENCE

Addison Wesley Longman Limited
Edinburgh Gate, Harlow
Essex CM20 2JE, England
and Associated Companies throughout the world

© Addison Wesley Longman Ltd 1999

The right of Brian Speed to be identified as author of this work has been asserted by him in accordance
with the Copyright, Designs and Patents Act 1988

First published 1999

British Library Cataloguing in Publication Data
A catalogue entry for this title is available from the British Library

ISBN 0-582-36916-9

Set by 30 in Stone $9\frac{1}{2}/11\frac{1}{2}$
Produced by Addison Wesley Longman Singapore (Pte) Ltd
Printed in Singapore

CONTENTS

ACKNOWLEDGEMENTS

I am indebted to the following Examination Groups for permission to use some of their GCSE questions in this book: EdExcel (London); Midlands Examining Group (MEG); Northern Examinations and Assessment Board (NEAB); Northern Ireland Schools Examinations and Assessment Council (NISEAC); Southern Examining Group (SEG).

WHAT IS A HOMEWORK HANDBOOK?

This Homework Handbook is a resource. It is for you, the student, to decide exactly how you use the book. The main purpose of this book is to help you when you are working by yourself – when you're researching or revising. It is designed to be extremely flexible, both in content and organization.

What's in this book

The Homework Handbook consists of hundreds of important mathematical terms, listed alphabetically.

- **Definitions, explanations and examples:** These terms all relate to key ideas in the most recent GCSE syllabuses. Each idea or topic is defined and concisely explained, and often incorporates worked examples and solutions to help you check your understanding.

- **Remember bubbles:** Many topics include extra hints, tips and comments, which may reinforce learning, highlight how different topics relate or let you know of common pitfalls.

- **Checkpoint questions:** Many of the topics include 'Checkpoints' – these are questions based on recent GCSE examination questions.

- **Checkpoint answers:** Once you have had a go at answering a Checkpoint, you can turn to the answers at the back of the book to see how you got on.

- **Cross-references:** Most topics are cross-referenced to other topics. This allows you to broaden and deepen your understanding of related themes. The cross-references also give you a chance to go back over the basic principles of themes with which you are having difficulty. Cross-references are easily identifiable:

- Either as words in bold italic type within the text:

  ...a change of *speed* or...

- Or as words following the 'compass' symbol at the end of an entry:

  ✛ *Congruent, Similar*

Using this book

- **Researching:** You can look up a particular term or topic just by finding it in the alphabetical list. Once you have the information you need, you can stop there; or your can follow up the related topics by using the cross-references; or you can work through a worked example or try a Checkpoint question, to see if you have fully understood the topic.

- **Revising:** For revision, you can really test your understanding of GCSE Mathematics by dipping into the Homework Handbook to check out terms and topics you are revising or have already revised.

GOOD LUCK!

MAKING THE MOST OF HOMEWORK AND REVISION

Why do you need to do homework anyway?

There are lots of reasons for doing homework. Each of these will apply to you at some stage, depending on the topic you are learning and how close you are to the examination:

- **Homework is your own work:** Homework allows you to work at your own speed, and often in your own place and at a time that is convenient to you.

- **Homework is a chance to catch up with work:** You need to catch up if you have missed some work, or if you are having difficulty understanding a topic.

- **Homework is a chance to follow up:** If you want to know more about a particular topic, or you are doing a project, you can use homework to deepen your understanding, or just to generate a few more ideas.

- **Homework is a chance to prepare:** You can get more out of your class time if you are prepared. You can also be ready to ask, or answer, questions more effectively.

- **Homework is a chance to consolidate:** You have seen a technique used in class – but do you remember it? Homework is a chance for you to work through problems and practise your mathematics.

- **Homework is revision time:** You will need to do more work on your own as the examinations approach. In particular, you need to gain experience in answering the sort of questions you will meet in the examination.

- **Homework develops useful skills:** Doing homework encourages useful (and sometimes difficult to maintain!) habits, like concentration, organization and self-discipline.

Planning and doing your homework and revision

The best (and probably only) way of doing homework is to work to a realistic but challenging plan. What do you need in order to achieve this? The most successful homework strategy is the one that works best for you. Here are some basic suggestions:

- **You need motivation:** It's easier and more effective (and more enjoyable) if your motivation is high. In other words, you should have a clear purpose, and be keen to achieve it. There are certain rewards that help you develop motivation. Examples are getting higher marks and understanding the subject better.

- **You need a weekly homework timetable:** Write out a weekly plan of your homework tasks. This plan may already be decided by deadlines for each subject. If you need to make your own plan, do a trial week first, to check that your workload is not too heavy (or too light).

- **You need to vary your homework:** Homework can consist of a series of different topics or subjects. This should keep you lively, alert and motivated.

- **You need to plan individual homework sessions for each topic or subject:** Each session should consist of fairly intensive work on a particular topic or subject. The session should not be too long (e.g. 30 minutes) and should have definite goals. Allow a break (e.g. five minutes) between sessions.

- **You need definite goals for each session:** For instance, you might have a specific piece of work which was set in class. You might want to re-read and add to your notes on a specific topic or practise answering a related examination question.

- **You need to be realistic:** Setting small, definite tasks increases your chances of completing them successfully. This should help with your confidence and motivation.

- **You need to be challenged:** If your task is too easy, you won't achieve much. Homework is a good example of 'no pain, no gain' – but that doesn't mean that homework has to be a chore!

- **You need to develop regular work habits:** This will avoid time-wasting periods of indecision, uncertainty and worry.

- **You need to adopt an active, not passive approach:** Learning is most effective when you are doing something. Summarizing information or answering a question is active. Reading through familiar notes can be quite passive, and possibly not very helpful (though it may seem like you're doing work!). Doing homework with a friend (e.g. testing each other) can work very well.

- **You need to give yourself rewards:** When you have achieved a certain number of objectives, why not reward yourself with a treat? This should help your motivation for the next series of tasks.

- **You need to take charge:** Revision is for *you* not your teacher. Remember it is what you learn that matters – and the more you learn, the better prepared you will be for the exam. So take charge!

Preparing for the examination

You should aim to complete most of your revision before the examinations actually start. Then you can spend any available time having a quick look at revision notes and relaxing between examinations. Here are some more tips, based on my experience as a teacher, examiner and student counsellor:

- **Avoid overworking:** This can be counterproductive, and can make you confused, tired and increasingly worried. Some anxiety is useful – it can give you 'positive anticipation' for the exam. However, too much anxiety can diminish your performance. You can manage anxiety by careful planning of your workload, and by various relaxation techniques.

- **Adopt a positive attitude to your work and yourself:** Careful revision helps you to prepare for the exams, and builds confidence.

- **Find out where your strengths and weaknesses are:** Remember that examiners are interested in what you can do, rather that what you cannot do. This should be your attitude too. Identify where you have difficulties in understanding, and work on those topics especially (even though it may be tempting just to avoid the problem areas).

- **Monitor your revision progress:** You could check off topics in your notes, in the syllabus or in this book, when you are confident of your understanding. Then move on to a new topic.

- **Concentrate on revision tasks, rather than yourself:** Deal with difficult topics as problems to be solved, not as evidence of your inability! However, you should also give yourself rewards when you have achieved particular goals.

- **Know when and where the examination will be held:** Also, confirm in advance what paper (including what tier) you are taking, and what sort of questions you can expect. Remember what equipment (a calculator, for instance) to take to the exam.

IN THE EXAMINATION

Five things to remember

- **Read the general instructions, and the questions, carefully:** Many candidates lost marks simply because they have misunderstood what they have to do.

- **Keep your answers concise, accurate and relevant:** If a question requires a written-out answer (in words) and you write a rambling, poorly organized answer you may lose marks and you will waste time. If possible, plan your answer (in your head) before you write it. Of course, if you need to produce a specific answer, do not forget to include your working.

- **Allocate your time according to the marks available:** Even before the exam, you can calculate approximately how many minutes to spend for each mark available. For example, if the total number of marks in a two-hour exam is 100, then each mark is 'worth' just over a minute of your time (you need to allow time for reading the question). If you spend ten minutes answering a five-mark question in that exam, you will have problems completing the exam in time.

- **Answer the questions you know you can do first:** This will build your confidence for the remainder of the exam. Also, if you run out of time (which should not happen!), you can at least be sure that all questions that you could have answered easily have been answered.

- **You should already know what to expect!** Before the exam, it is important to make sure that you are already familiar with the types of question you are likely to face. These will vary between examining boards, syllabuses and papers, and will also depend on the tier you are studying.

Marking scheme

- **Mark allocation:** The written (terminal) examination in GCSE Mathematics may provide 80 per cent of your total assessment (the rest is either coursework or the problem solving paper).

- **Mark distribution:** Within the written examinations, marks are distributed as follows:

  - **Foundation tier** (each paper, out of 100 marks):
    Approx. 35 marks are for number work.
    Approx. 15 marks are for algebra.
    Approx. 25 marks are for shape and space work.
    Approx. 25 marks are for data handling.

  - **Intermediate tier** (each paper, out of 100 marks):
    Approx. 25 marks are for number work.
    Approx. 25 marks are for algebra.
    Approx. 25 marks are for shape and space work.
    Approx. 25 marks are for data handling.

  - **High tier**:
    Approx. 15 marks are for number work.
    Approx. 35 marks are for algebra.
    Approx. 25 marks are for shape and space work.
    Approx. 25 marks are for data handling.

Types of questions

Make sure you know your calculator; you will be expected to make good use of it. However, note that one of your papers will be a 'non-calculator' paper in which you cannot use a calculator. Make sure you know which paper this is, and be ready for the arithmetic you will have to do yourself.

Structured questions

These are the most common form of question; some examination boards only use structured questions.

The basic format is to break the question down into sections (a), (b), (c), etc. Often, related parts of the question are grouped together, so that section (a) might be further broken down into subsections (i), (ii), (iii) and so on.

Often groups of questions follow on from each other; this makes it very important to get the first part right! It is usual for structured questions to become more demanding as you work through them.

Unstructured questions

On each paper you will find at least one unstructured question which expects you to recognise all the necessary stages which are involved. You can recognise these questions because:

- They are not split in sections.

- There are quite a few marks available (3 or more).

- There are quite a few lines for you to write your answer in.

This type of question needs to be read carefully (more than once!) and you will need to think about the order in which you need to do things. You will certainly need to calculate at least one intermediate step before being able to give an answer. For example:

Russell and Jane are twins taking their driving test. The probability that Russell will pass is estimated to be 0.6. The probability that Jane will pass is estimated to be 0.85. Calculate the probability that only one of the twins will pass their test.

First you need to be able to interpret the question – here you have to find the probability of *either* Russell *or* Jane passing (one but not both). You could perhaps construct a tree diagram to work out all the possibilities, before finally identifying the correct values and adding them together to find the answer.

Questions requiring reasons

These will be questions asking you to give not only an answer, but also some reasons justifying that answer. You do not need to write an essay, but do need to provide concise, unambiguous reasons.

If the Examiner cannot tell what it is you are trying to say you will not get the marks. For example:

Paul decides to use a questionnaire to find out how pupils at the school use the library. Paul gives the pupils a questionnaire when he stamps their books.

Is this a suitable way to give out questionnaires? Give a reason for your answer.

ACCELERATION

This is the rate of change of **speed** or velocity with respect to time. The standard unit is metres per second per second (m/s^2). The **gradient** on a velocity/time graph will represent the acceleration.

> Remember: If the velocity/time graph is curved, you will need to find the gradient of a tangent in order to find acceleration.

-+- **Gradient**

ACCURACY

Accuracy often depends on **rounding** off an answer to the correct number of **significant figures** or **decimal places**. You could be asked to round off to the nearest penny or cm, etc., in which case you round off to the nearest *whole number*. You will find that some questions will ask you to round off to a *particular degree* of accuracy, while others do not.

Number	Significant figures		
	1	2	3
13,947	10,000	14,000	13,900
46.85	50	47	46.9
0.004193	0.004	0.0042	0.00419

Number	Decimal places		
	1	2	3
26.4791	26.5	26.48	26.479
0.0815	0.1	0.08	0.082
5.1972	5.2	5.20	5.197

If the question *does* ask for a particular degree of accuracy, then simply do that. But, if the question does *not* state anything about accuracy, then you have to round off to what you decide is a *sensible* answer. If you are in doubt, then a good guide is to round off to *one more significant figure* than the figures used in the question. For example:

● Find the area of the rectangle 5.6 cm by 9.7 cm.

Since the numbers given in the question are both to *two* significant figures, round off to *three significant figures*. In this case your answer should be 54.3 cm².

Of course there are some situations in which common sense should tell you that the answer must be a whole number:

● How many days will a tin of cocoa last?

● How many sheep can you get in a particular size pen?

Never round off *too soon*, especially when there are a number of stages to be worked out, as this will usually result in an inaccurate final answer.

Always *check* your answer to see if it is sensible and that it is rounded off to a suitable degree of accuracy. Questions will not usually examine rounding off as a topic in itself, but it will be included in quite a few questions throughout your examination. Unless you round off correctly in these questions you will lose marks.

> Remember: A safeguard against being inaccurate is to show all the stages in your **method of solution**. You will then get the majority of marks even if you make an arithmetical mistake in your calculation.

Exam Question
The size of the crowd at a football match is given as 24,600 to the nearest hundred.

(a) What is the lowest number that the crowd could be?
(b) What is the largest number that the crowd could be?

Solution
(a) 24,550
(b) 24,649 – We would not use the upper bound here because we are dealing with integers only and so would not use 24,649.99999

CHECKPOINT

Round off 45.17

(a) To one significant figure.
(b) To two significant figures.
(c) To one decimal place.

-+- **Rounding**

ADDING/ADDITION

-+- **Directed numbers**

ADJACENT

Adjacent means 'next to'. In the case of a right-angled triangle we are often concerned with finding the *adjacent side*. This is often easiest to find by *eliminating* two of the three sides:

- Eliminate the **hypotenuse** – the side opposite the right angle.
- Eliminate the *side opposite* the angle in question.
- The remaining side is the *adjacent side*.

In the left-hand diagram, the angle in question is CÂB. The *side adjacent* to CÂB is therefore AC. In the right-hand diagram, the angle in question is AĈB. The *side adjacent* to AĈB is therefore AC. Notice how the adjacent side is the one next to *both* the right angle and the angle of the question.

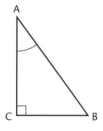
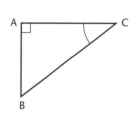

ALGEBRA

Algebra is the part of mathematics that uses letters for numbers. It is a large topic that includes **solving** equations, **factorizing**, **transforming equations**, **generalizing**, using **formulae** and **substitution**. Algebra is used at all levels of GCSE mathematics – simple algebra at the Foundation Level and more complicated algebra at the Higher Level.

One of the most important things in GCSE algebra questions is to recognize that the question *is* about algebra. Many questions now use the *words* rather than the letters, so you need to *recognize* that expressing the information given in the form of a simple equation will help solve the problem. Take the following question at Foundation Level:

Exam Question
In his will Ken leaves all his estate to be shared among three people. Alice is to have £3,000 more than Brian. Cyril is to have four times as much as Brian.

(a) If Cyril received £8,000, how much would Alice get?
(b) When Ken died, Alice and Cyril received the same amount of money. How much was Ken's estate?

Solution
This is an algebra-type question that can best be solved by using simple equations. For instance:

If Brian receives £x
Alice will get $x + 3,000$
Cyril will get $4x$

(a) If $4x = 8,000$
 Then $x = 2,000$
 Hence Alice gets $2,000 + 3,000 = £5,000$

(b) Where $4x = x + 3,000$
 $3x = 3,000$
 $x = 1,000$

This means that Alice received £4,000, Brian £1,000 and Cyril £4,000. So altogether they received £9,000, the value of Ken's estate.

The major mistake students made with this question was in *not recognizing* that it was an algebra-type question and trying to solve it by trial and error rather than using simple equations. Trial and error takes longer, often leads to wrong answers and scores few marks for method.

> *Remember: The Intermediate and Higher Level GCSE examination papers will have quite a few questions in them that use algebra.*

Exam Question
The cost, C pence, of making a clown's hat in the shape of the cone shown, with radius r cm and slant height l cm, is given by the formula:

$$C = 2\pi r + \pi r l$$

(Rounded off to the nearest penny.)

(a) Fully factorize the right-hand side of the equation.
(b) Hence, or otherwise, transform the formula to make r the subject.
(c) Hence, or otherwise, find the radius of a clown's hat with a slant height of 18 cm and costing £4.40.

(NEAB; I)

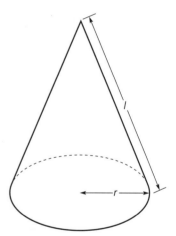

Solution
(a) $C = \pi r (2 + l)$

(b) $r = \dfrac{C}{\pi (2 + l)}$

(c) When $C = 440$, $l = 18$, then $r = \dfrac{440}{\pi (2 + 18)} = 7.0028$
 A sensible rounding is 7 cm.

Exam Question
The diagram shows a cuboid with length l, width w, and height h.

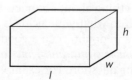

Write in its simplest form an expression for the total surface area of the cuboid in terms of l, w and h.

Solution
$2lw + 2wh + 2lh = 2 (lw + wh + lh)$

ALGEBRAIC FRACTIONS

These are *fractions* that have letters in them, e.g.
$\frac{3}{x}$, $\frac{y+3}{5-y}$ They will only be found in the higher levels
of mathematics and usually in the form of equations
to solve. For example:

$$\frac{3}{x} + \frac{2}{x+1} = 1$$

$$\frac{3(x+1) + 2x}{x(x+1)} = 1 \qquad \text{get a common denominator}$$

$3(x+1) + 2x = x(x+1)$ cross multiply
$\qquad 5x + 3 = x^2 + x$ expand
$\qquad x^2 - 4x - 3 = 0$ simplify

You would now solve this *quadratic* equation.

ALLIED ANGLES

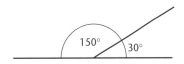

Transversal

ALTERNATE ANGLES

Transversal

'AND' RULE

The 'AND' rule comes from the topic of *probability*.
To find the probability of event A *and* event B, the
probability of each event is *multiplied* together. For
example:

> A drawer contains five green socks and four yellow
> socks. What is the probability of picking out a pair
> of green socks one dark night when you can't see
> the colours properly?

The probability of the first sock being green is $\frac{5}{9}$
The probability of the second sock being green is $\frac{4}{8}$
Hence the probability of both the first *and* second
socks being green is

$$\frac{5}{9} \times \frac{4}{8} = \frac{20}{72} = \frac{5}{18}$$

The most common error to be made in this is to add
the fractions instead of *multiplying* them.

> Remember: AND will mean multiply.

CHECKPOINT

What is the probability of rolling three sixes in a row?

ANGLE

Angle is the amount of turn, and is measured in
degrees.

Types of angle

● A *right* angle is a quarter turn, or 90°.

● An *acute* angle is less than 90°.

● An *obtuse* angle is greater than 90°, but less than
180°.

● A *reflex* angle is greater than 180°, but less than
360°.

Facts about angles

● Angles on a straight line add up to 180°.

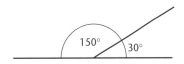

● Vertically opposite angles are equal.

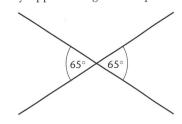

● Angles around a point add up to 360°.

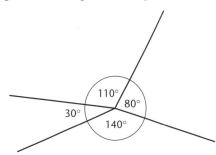

● The three angles in a *triangle* add up to 180°.

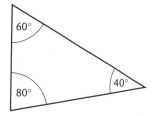

● The N angles inside an N-sided *polygon* will *add
up* to 180° (N–2)°. These angles are called the
interior angles.

● The *N exterior angles* of an *N*-sided polygon will *add up* to 360°.

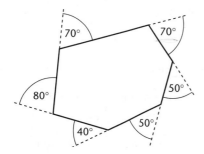

● The size of *each interior angle* in a regular *N*-sided polygon is given by $180° - \dfrac{360°}{N}$

> Remember: In a regular Polygon – the interior angle and the exterior angle will always add up to 180°.

● The size of each exterior angle in a regular *N*-sided polygon is given by $\dfrac{360°}{N}$

● From any ***chord*** in a circle there are many *triangles* that can be formed in the same segment that touch the circumference, as shown. All these angles from the same chord are *equal*.

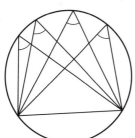

● From any ***chord*** in a circle, there is only one *triangle* that can be drawn to the centre of the circle. The angle (2*x*°) subtended at the centre is twice the size of any angle subtended at the circumference (*x*°) in the same segment as the centre.

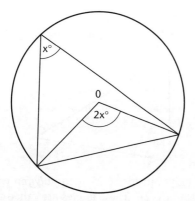

● Any ***quadrilateral*** drawn so that the four vertices touch the circumference of the same circle is

called *cyclic* and its *opposite angles* add up to 180°, as shown in the diagram below.

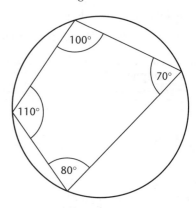

● If you draw any ***triangle*** in a semi-circle where one of the sides is the diameter, as in the diagram below, then the angle at the circumference is a *right angle*.

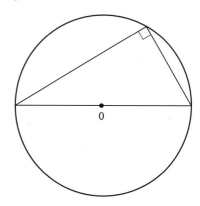

Exam Question

The accompanying diagram (which is not to scale) represents three sets of parallel lines. State the size of:

(a)   angle *a*
(b)   angle *b*
(c)   angle *c*

(NEAB; I)

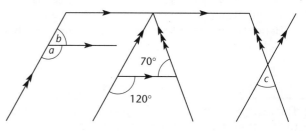

Solution
(a)   *a* = 120°
(b)   *b* = 180 – 120 = 60°
(c)   *c* = 180 – (70 + 60) = 50°

Angle of depression

This is the angle that a line makes with a horizontal line *looking down*; this is the angle A shown in the next diagram.

Angle of elevation

This is the angle that a line makes with the horizontal *looking up*; this is angle B shown.

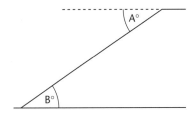

Angle of depression (A) and angle of elevation (B)

Angle of rotation

This is the angle that a shape *turns through* in a transformation called a **rotation**.

> Remember: If a negative angle is used, the rotation is anticlockwise. If a positive angle is used, the rotation is clockwise.

APPROXIMATE

The 'intelligent' guess at an answer to some mathematical problem. It is often found by **rounding** the data off, then by working out a simple problem. For example:

A family went from Bude in Cornwall to York in Yorkshire, a distance of 483 miles, in 7 hours 15 minutes. What was the average speed?

Round 483 off to 490 and the time to 7 hours to give a speed of 490/7 = 70 mph.

In a question that specifically asks you for an *approximate* answer you ought to be able to show *how* you obtained your answer by either rounding off and doing the problem, or doing the problem and then rounding off. Of course an approximate answer should not be given to too many significant figures.

Exam Question
Do not use a calculator when answering this question. All working must be shown.

Obtain an *estimate* for $\dfrac{619 \times 93}{41}$.

Solution
Round off each number to one significant figure, to give

$\dfrac{600 \times 90}{40}$

The 40 cancels with the 600 to give 15×90
Which is just below $15 \times 100 = 1500$
So an estimate of the answer can be 1500.

ARC

An arc is the curved part of a sector, as shown, where O is the centre of a circle, and OA and OB are both radiuses (radii) of the circle. The *arc length* is calculated with the formula:

$$\text{arc length} = \frac{X}{360}\,\pi D$$

Where *D* is the diameter of the circle, and *X* is the angle of the sector.

Questions that use this formula will appear on the Higher Level papers only.

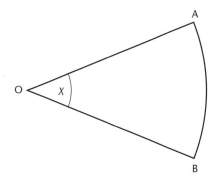

Arc

AREA

Area is the amount of space inside a flat two-dimensional (2D) shape, and is measured in squares, e.g. square centimetres or square metres.

Common areas

- Area of **rectangle** = length × breadth.
- Area of **triangle** = $\frac{1}{2}$ × base length × height.
- Area of **parallelogram** = base length × height.
- Area of **trapezium** = average length of parallel sides × perpendicular distance between them.
- Area of **circle** = πr^2, where *r* is the radius.
- Area of **sector** = $\dfrac{x\pi r^2}{360}$ where *x* is the angle of the sector.

There will be quite a few examination questions on this topic every year and at every level. These formulae may be given to you on a *formula sheet* so do ensure that you are familiar with the formula given by your examination group.

Exam Question
A logo consists of an equilateral triangle, whose side is of length 4 cm, and three circular arcs, whose centres are the vertices of the triangle.

(a) Find the total area of the region bounded by the three arcs, giving your answer correct to three significant figures.

(b) Given that the length of each side of the equilateral triangle is 4x cm, find an expression for the area in terms of x.

(NEAB; H)

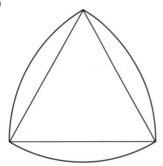

Solution
(a) The area of the triangle is found by ($\frac{1}{2}$ × base × height) giving ($\frac{1}{2}$ × 4 × 4 × sin 60° = 6.9282).
Each segment = sector area – triangle area
Where the sector area = $\frac{60}{360}$ × π × 4 × 4 = 8.37758
Hence segment area = 1.44938
So the total area = 3 × segment + triangle = 11.3 cm².
(b) A shape with said side of 4x is a similar shape with length ratio of 1:x, hence the area ratio is 1:x²
Hence area of new shape will be 11.3 × x² = 11.3x²

Exam Question
A factory produces badges by stamping discs from rectangular sheets of plastic.
Each sheet of plastic is 30 cm long and 25 cm wide.
The diameter of each disc is 4 cm.
The diagram shows part of a sheet with discs cut from it.

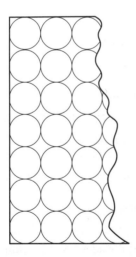

(a) How many discs can be cut from one sheet of plastic?
(b) What is the area of one sheet of plastic?
(c) What is the area of one disc?
(d) The plastic left after the discs are cut out is wasted. What percentage of each sheet of plastic is wasted?

Solution
(a) You could fit 7 down the length and 6 along the width, giving a total of 42
(b) 30 × 25 = 750 cm²
(c) π × 2² = 12.57 cm² (rounded)
(d) waste = 750 – (42 × 12.566371) = 222.21243
% waste = $\frac{222.21243}{750}$ × 100 = 29.6%

ARITHMETIC MEAN

⊹ *Mean*

ASYMPTOTE/ASYMPTOTIC

Usually refers to a graph where the curve gets nearer and nearer to a straight line (usually one axis) but never quite touches that line. A **hyperbola**, for example, has two asymptotes. (High level only.)

⊹ *Graphs, reciprocal equations*

AURAL TESTS

An aural test is one in which you have to listen to the questions and then answer them. You do not have a printed paper with the questions on. You need mental arithmetic or a quick pen and pencil routine, since you will not be allowed to use your calculator. The question will usually be read out twice and slowly so that you can jot down some information. Jot down the necessary *figures*, but as few *words* as possible, since you do need to be *listening* to the whole question. For example:
Each question will be read out twice, slowly. Then you will be given one minute in which to arrive at your answer and to write it down.

1. A rectangle measures 9 cm by 4 cm. A square has the same area. What is the perimeter of this square?
2. What is the cost of 30 square metres of lino at £4.50 per square metre?
3. A salesman earns 2% commission on sales of £3,000. What is his commission in pounds?
4. The average cost of 6 drinks is 92p. What is the total cost?
5. If one unit of gas cost 27p, what is the cost in pounds of 300 units?
6. A revision guide is 1.5 cm thick. How many of these books can be placed on the shelves of a bookshop if the shelves are one metre long?
7. Which of the following is the nearest to the average height of a woman in Europe: 98 cm; 160 cm; 198 cm?

Not many exam boards use these at the moment, but it is a good skill to practice.

AVERAGE

What people usually mean by the average is the 'middle thing' or the thing that most people have. There are three different types of average:

Mode

This is what most people have or do, or the most frequently appearing item of data. For example, the record that is currently number 1 in the charts is the one that has sold the most during the previous week, so it is the *mode* or the modal record.

Median

This is the 'middle' item of data once it has all been put into a specific order. For example, if you had nine people and wanted to find their *median* height, then you would put them into the order of their heights; whoever is in the middle then has the median height. If you need to find the median of an *even* set of numbers, then you need the arithmetic mean of the *middle two* numbers.

> *Remember: The arithmetic mean of two numbers is found by adding them and dividing the result by 2.*

Mean (arithmetic mean)

This is the average that most people are familiar with and really intend when they use the word 'average'. It is found by adding up all the data and dividing it by the number of data items you added up. For example, from the numbers 1,2,3,4,4,5,5,5,5

the **mode** will be 5 (the number occurring most often)

the **median** will be 4 (the middle number, with numbers arranged in order)

the **mean** will be 3.78 (34/9, i.e. the total divided by the 9 items of data)

The most common mistake to make with averages is to calculate the wrong type; so do learn the difference between each type of average.

Exam Question

Two dice were thrown together 125 times. The scores obtained are shown in the table. Use this information to find:

(a) the mode of the scores,
(b) the median score,
(c) the mean score.

(NEAB; F)

Score	Frequency
2	4
3	7
4	9
5	11
6	7
7	5
8	17
9	19
10	24
11	12
12	10

Solution

(a) The mode is the most common, hence the 10.
(b) The median is the
$$\frac{125 + 1}{2} = 63\text{rd number,}$$
so counting down to the 63rd number you come to 9.
(c) The mean score is calculated as: $(2 \times 4) + (3 \times 7) + (4 \times 9) + (5 \times 11) + (6 \times 7) + (7 \times 5) + (8 \times 17) + (9 \times 19) + (10 \times 24) + (11 \times 12) + (12 \times 10)$ all divided by 125. This is $996 \div 125 = 8.0$ (rounded off).

Exam Question

The fifteen grandmothers at a Darby and Joan club noted how many grandchildren they all had. It was

6, 7, 3, 8, 7, 6, 3, 5, 4, 6, 3, 7, 5, 4, 7

Find
(a) the mode
(b) the median
(c) the mean.

Solution

(a) The number that occurs the most is number 7
(b) Rearrange the numbers into order, find the middle, which is 6
(c) Add all the numbers together, to get 81, divide by the number of numbers, which is 15, to get 5.4

CHECKPOINT

For: 2,8,1,5,7,6,5,3,2,2,7

State:
(a) the mode
(b) the median
(c) the mean

AXES

The lines on which we put numbers on a graph are called the axes. Usually:

● The *horizontal* line is called the *x*-axis.

● The *vertical* line is called the *y*-axis.

AXIS OF SYMMETRY

An axis of summary is the line that a three-dimensional shape rotates around to demonstrate **rotational symmetry**. Examples are shown in the accompanying diagram.

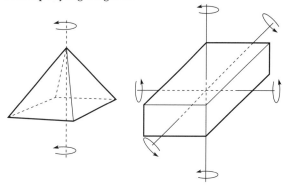

BAR CHART

A bar chart is a display of information using bars of different *lengths* to represent the frequency of items of data. The one shown represents how many babies were born in one week at Jessop's hospital in Sheffield.

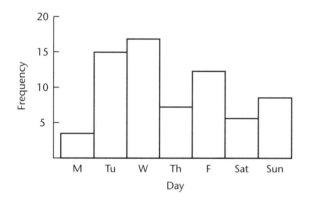

BASE NUMBER

A number which is raised to some index or exponent, e.g. in 5^3, the base number is 5.

 Index

BEARINGS

Look at a compass similar to the one shown; you may well see numbers like 005°, 070°, 340°, etc. These are 3-figure *bearings* and represent the *clockwise angle from due north* which that direction is making. You should see that east is 090°, south is 180°, south west is 225° etc. The most common error to make in bearings is to measure anticlockwise instead of clockwise.

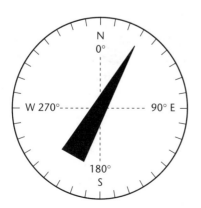

Back bearings

If the bearing from A to B is known, then the bearing back from B to A can be calculated by adding on 180°. If the back bearing is calculated as greater than 360°, then subtract 360° from the final answer for the correct bearing.

> *Remember: To find a back bearing you will either add 180° or subtract 180°, whichever gives an answer between 0 and 360.*

Exam Question
A ship sails from point A on a bearing of 035° to point B, 50 km away. From B it then sails 80 km due south to point C.

(a) Using a scale of 1 cm to represent 10 km, make a scale drawing of the ship's course.
(b) Use your scale drawing to find the distance, in km, from A to C in a straight line.
(c) From your scale drawing find the bearing of C from A.
(d) Calculate the distance from A to C in a straight line.

(NEAB; I)

Solution
(a) You should have drawn the ship's journey using ruler and protractor.
(b) 48.5 km.
(c) 144°.
(d) Use a combination of trigonometry and Pythagoras, applied to the right-angled triangles formed with point D, the perpendicular of A to DC.

Then
$$BD = 50 \sin 55° = 40.96$$
$$AD = 50 \cos 55° = 28.68$$
$$DC = 80 - BD = 39.04$$
$$AC^2 = AD^2 + DC^2 = 2346.8$$
$$AC = \sqrt{(2346.8)}$$
$$= 48.44 \text{ km}$$

Exam Question
Hotten is 8 miles due North of Kirrin.
Budle is 14 miles due East of Hotten.

(a) Draw a sketch to show the relative positions of Hotten, Kirrin and Budle.
(b) Write down the three figure bearing of Hotten from Budle.
(c) Calculate the direct distance from Kirrin to Budle.

Solution
(a)
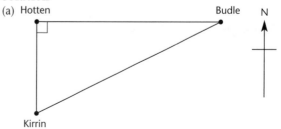

(b) This is due west, which is 270°
(c) Use Pythagoras as $x^2 = 8^2 + 14^2$
$$= 260$$
$$x = \sqrt{260} = 16.1 \text{ miles (rounded)}.$$

CHECKPOINT
Tully is on a bearing of 138° from Ross. On what bearing is Ross from Tully?

BEST BUY

You face a best-buy problem when there are alternatives and you have the choice of which to buy. The usual technique is to find either the *weight per penny* (or £1) of each item or the *cost per unit weight* (or length, or area, etc.). This choice will usually depend on the information presented. The best buy will then be either the one that gives you the most weight etc. for each unit of money, or cost least per unit of weight etc.

> *Remember: You find weight per cost by dividing weight by cost. You find cost per weight by dividing cost by weight.*

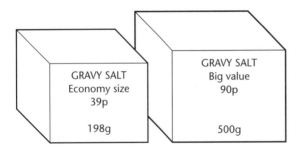

Exam Question

Gravy salt is sold in two different sized packets as shown.

(a) What is the weight of the gravy salt per penny
    (i) for the 'Economy' packet?
    (ii) for the 'Big value' packet?
(b) From your answer to part (a), which packet is the better value, and why?

(NEAB; I)

Solution

(a) (i) 198g ÷ 39 = 5.0769... g
    (ii) 500g ÷ 90 = 5.555... g
(b) The 'big value' is the better buy because you get more weight for your money.

BISECT

Bisect means to put into two equal halves. It is most commonly used in **constructions** as one of the following:

Bisect a line

To bisect the line AB, set your pair of compasses to about three quarters of the length of line AB, and

with the sharp point at one end draw a faint semi-circle; then repeat from the other end, keeping the compass arc the same length. You need to find out where the two semi-circles cross over. The straight line between these points will give the line bisector.

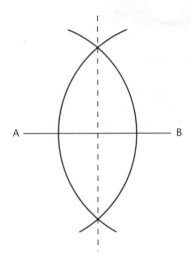

> *Remember: Always make your construction lines much fainter than the other lines.*

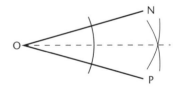

To bisect the angle NOP, with your compasses set at about 2 cm, put the sharp end at the vertex of the angle 0, and arc the angle as shown with a faint line. At both points where this arc cuts the *sides* of the angle, and using the sharp end of the compasses, draw another faint arc across the angle as shown. Where these last two arcs *cross*, join to the vertex at 0. The resulting line is the *angle bisector*.

    An examination question will use the words 'with compass and pencil only, construct...'. You then must construct the bisectors as shown, or gain no marks at all. By all means check your accuracy afterwards with a protractor or ruler and redraw if you are not accurate. Also do remember to show your construction lines clearly and not to rub them out or to draw them so faint that no one can see them.

> *Remember: If a question asks you to draw. . . then you may use a protractor. If it says 'construct' you should **not** use the protractor.*

BODMAS

This is a mnemonic which helps us remember what to work out first in an arithmetical situation where there seems to be several ways of proceeding. It stands for the phrase:

Brackets, Of, Division, Multiplication, Addition, Subtraction.

We do these things in that order. For example:

$$3 \times 4 + \tfrac{1}{2} \text{ of } 12 \div 3 - (9 - 7)$$

is done in the order:

● Brackets	3	$\times 4$	$+$	$\tfrac{1}{2}$ of 12	$\div 3$	$- 2$
● Of	3	$\times 4$	$+$	6	$\div 3$	$- 2$
● Division	3	$\times 4$	$+$	2		$- 2$
● Multiplication	12		$+$	2		$- 2$
● Addition			14			$- 2$
● Subtraction				12		

BRACKETS

We often need to make sure that in a formula certain numbers are calculated first. We do this by the use of brackets. For example in the formula $C = \tfrac{5}{9} \times (F - 32)$, it is important to subtract the 32 from F before doing anything else. If a bracket appears in a formula or an expression to work out, then *always work out the bracket first*.

Exam Question
Place brackets in the following statements to make them true.

(a) $6 \div 3 + 5 \times 4 = 3$
(b) $6 - 2 \times 5 + 4 = 36$

Solution
(a) $6 \div (3 + 5) \times 4 = 3$
(b) $(6 - 2) \times (5 + 4) = 36$

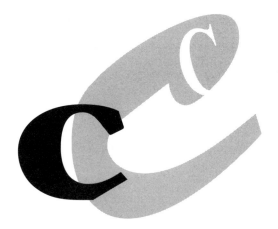

CALCULATOR

After the year 2000 all GCSE examinations will allow you to have your calculator with you for one of the written papers and for the coursework assignments. The questions on the papers where you are allowed a calculator will be set on the assumption that you have got a suitable calculator with you. The calculator is the responsibility of the *candidate* and not the school, so candidates need to supply their own, together with spare batteries if required. Always try to use a *familiar* calculator, since there may be considerable differences between models. You do not want the extra pressure of learning to use a calculator in a timed situation.

When using a calculator in the examination, do not forget to write down any *method of solution* that is relevant. Otherwise marks could be lost if the answer is wrong and no method of solution can be seen. Try also to keep as accurate an answer in the calculator as you can for multiple-stage calculations; any rounding off should be done at the final stage. If you round off too early, your final answer will be less accurate.

CANCELLING

This is what we call the process when a fraction is divided top and bottom by a particular **integer** (whole number). For example, $\frac{9}{15}$ cancels to $\frac{3}{5}$ by dividing both top and bottom by 3.

CARTESIAN GRID

-♦- *Graph*

CENTRE OF ENLARGEMENT

-♦- *Enlargement*

CHARTS

An important part of the GCSE examinations is the inclusion of charts that are a familiar sight in everyday life.

Conversion chart

A conversion chart from litres to gallons, and of course the other way round, is shown.

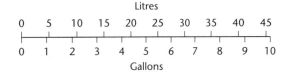

Information chart

The first chart shown (below) needs to be read carefully to provide information. You would read this particular chart to find out the details about certain monsters in the game of Dungeons and Dragons.

Monster	Size	To Hit A.C.0	Armor class	Hit dice	No. of attacks	Damage per attack
Diplodocus	L	7	6	24	1	3–18
Elasmosauras	L	8	7	15	1	4–24
Gargosaurus	L	9	5	13	3	1–3/1–3/7–28
Iguanadon	L	13	4	6	3	1–3/1–3/2–8
Lambeosaurus	L	9	6	12	1	2–12
Megalosaurus	L	9	5	12	1	3–18
Monoclonius	L	12	3/4	8	1	2–16
Mosasaurus	L	9	7	12	1	4–32
Paleascincus	L	12	–3	9	1	2–12
Pentaceratops	L	9	2/6	12	3	1–6/1–10/1–10
Plateosaurus	L	12	5	8	nil	nil
Plesiosaurus	L	7	7	20	1	5–20
Pteranodon	L	16	7	3+3	1	2–8
Stegosaurus	L	7	2/5	18	1	5–20
Styracosaurus	L	10	2/4	10	1	2–16
Teratosaurus	L	10	5	10	3	1–3/1–3/3–18
Triceratops	L	7	2/6	16	3	1–8/1–12/1–12
Tyrannosaurus rex	L	7	5	18	3	1–6/1–6/5–40

The second chart shown is another information chart, telling you the various costs of staying at a hotel for each week during the year.

Basic holiday price in £s per person – Gatwick departures						
Between	9 May 12 June		13 June 24 July		25 July 5 September	
Number of nights	7	14	7	14	7	14
Hotel Knowle	211	319	219	328	224	367
Hotel Hildaro	193	276	197	285	204	294
Addition for Heathrow departure £30 per person Addition for sea views £1.90 per person per night Addition for insurance cover £4.75 per person No reduction for children or OAPs						

Questions involving charts mainly appear at Foundation level but could also appear on the Intermediate and Higher Level papers.

 Pie chart

CHORD

Any straight line drawn in a circle from one part of the circumference to another is called a chord. As you can see in the figure shown, a chord divides a circle into two segments, the larger one called the *major segment* and the smaller one the *minor segment*.

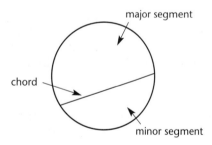

 Angles

CIRCLES

A circle is the locus of a point that is always the same distance from a given point which is the centre of that circle. You should learn the terms associated with circles, as detailed below and labelled on the figure:

● The outside edge of the circle is called the **circumference**.

● Any line from the centre of the circle to the circumference is called a **radius**.

● Any line through the centre of a circle from circumference to circumference is called a **diameter**.

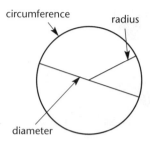

● The *length of the circumference* of a circle (**perimeter**) is given by the formula:

circumference = π × diameter

● The *area* of a circle is given by the formula:

area = π × (radius)²

Angles in a circle

Angles, pi(π)

Exam Question

In a computer game, a ghost eats circles and triangles. Each time it eats a circle its brightness is increased by 5 watts per cm² of circle area eaten.

(a) A game is played and the ghost eats twelve circles each of radius 0.5 cm
  (i) What is the area of each circle?
  (ii) By how much has the brightness of the ghost increased after eating all the twelve circles?
(b) Each time a ghost eats a triangle its brightness is decreased by $\frac{2}{5}$ of its brightness.
  A ghost starts a game with a brightness of 50 watts. What would its brightness be after it had eaten three triangles?

(NEAB; I)

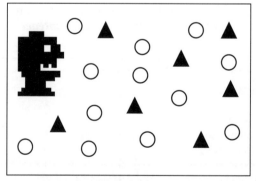

Ghost eating circles and triangles

Solution
(a) (i) π × (0.5)² = 0.78 cm² (or 0.79)
  (ii) 0.78 × 12 × 5 = 47.1 watts (using unrounded 0.78...)
(b) 50 × $\frac{3}{5}$ × $\frac{3}{5}$ × $\frac{3}{5}$ = 10.8 watts.

CHECKPOINT

Write down the formula involving radius for:

(a) The circumference of a circle.
(b) The area of a circle.

CIRCUMFERENCE

The circumference of a *circle* is the outside edge and is calculated by the formula:

circumference = π × diameter

The circumference is often also quoted with the formula:

circumference = 2 × π × radius

Both these formulae will give the same length of circumference and a common error is to mix the two together.

Exam Question
A bicycle wheel has a diameter of 90 cm.
Approximately how many revolutions would the wheel make in covering 2 miles? (8 km = 5 miles)

Solution
Circumference of the wheel is π × 90 = 282.74334 cm
2 miles = (8 ÷ 5) × 2 = 3.2 kilometres
       = 3.2 × 1,000 × 100 = 320,000 cm
number of revolutions = 320,000 ÷ 282.74334 = 1,131.7685.
The approximate answer will be either 1,130 or 1,100.

COEFFICIENT

A coefficient is the number in front of a letter or group of letters in an algebraic term. For example in $3x$, the 3 is the coefficient of x. In $5xy$ the 5 is the coefficient of xy. The coefficient is multiplied by the letters.

COMBINED EVENTS

A combined event is part of *probability*, where two or more events are happening at the same time. The two main situations which are examined at GCSE are concerned with the AND rule and the OR rule:

- **AND** is the type where both events happen at the same time. To find this combined probability we multiply the probabilities of each single event.

- **OR** is the type when either one event or the other can happen, but not both at the same time. To find this probability we add the probabilities of each event.

The events must all be part of a sample space, that is to say a situation that takes account of *all* possible outcomes. This is often illustrated on a *tree diagram*.

> *Remember: AND means multiply*
> *OR means add*

Exam Question
A bag contains 7 toffees and 3 mints.

(a) What is the probability that a sweet taken from the bag at random will be a toffee?
(b) Another bag contains 5 fruit drops and 7 mints. Helen takes one sweet from each bag without looking. Draw a tree diagram to show the possible outcomes and their probabilities.
(c) What is the probability that Helen takes
    (i) two mints
    (ii) exactly one mint?

Solution
(a) $\frac{7}{10}$
(b)

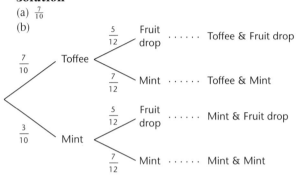

(c) (i) $\frac{3}{10} \times \frac{7}{12} = \frac{21}{120}$ or $\frac{7}{40}$ (or 0.175)
    (ii) Toffee and mint or mint and fruit drop
    $\frac{7}{10} \times \frac{7}{12} + \frac{3}{10} \times \frac{5}{12} = \frac{64}{120} = \frac{8}{15}$ (or 0.533)

COMMON FACTORS

Common factors are the factors that two or more *integers* or whole numbers have in common. For example, the common factors of 18, 24 and 36 are 1, 2, 3, and 6. Here, 6 is the **highest common factor** (HCF).

COMMON MULTIPLES

Common multiples are the multiples that two or more *integers* or whole numbers have in common. For example, some common multiples of 5 and 3 are 15, 30, 45,... Here, 15 is the **lowest common multiple** (LCM).

> *CHECKPOINT*
>
> Write down:
>
> (a) The HCF of 24 and 32
> (b) The LCM of 15 and 35

COMPLEMENT

The complement of an event A is the event where A does not happen.
   If an event A has a probability of $P(A)$, then the probability of the complement of A is $1 - P(A)$. For example, if the probability of Joseph winning is 0.7, then the probability of Joseph not winning will be $1 - 0.7 = 0.3$

COMPOUND INTEREST

This is the type of interest most likely to be paid by banks and building societies. It is a system that allows your interest to grow, giving interest on the interest. For example:

> To find the compound interest on £150 at a rate of 8% per annum (that is per year) for 3 years.
>
> At the end of 1 year, interest = $150 \times \frac{8}{100}$ = £12
> So total amount after 1 year = £150 + £12 = £162
> End of 2nd year interest = $162 \times \frac{8}{100}$ = £12.96
> So total after 2 years = £162 + £12.96 = £174.96
> End of 3rd year interest = $174.96 \times \frac{8}{100}$ = £14.00
> (rounded to nearest penny).

The most efficient way to calculate compound interest is:

> where R is the interest rate,
> where N is the number of times the rate is to be applied,
> where P is the principal amount started off with,

then the *final amount* is given by $P \times (1 + \frac{R}{100})^N$. To find the *interest paid*, simply subtract the original amount from the final amount.

> *Remember: The formula $Px (1 + \frac{R}{100})^N$ is the quickest way to calculate compound interest.*

Exam Question
Elsie won £60 in a beauty contest and put it into a building society account that paid 8% compound interest annually. How much would she have in this account if the money were left there for 3 years?

Solution
$R = 8$
$N = 3$
$P = £60$
Final amount = $P \times (1 + \frac{R}{100})^N$
$= 60 \times (1 + \frac{8}{100})^3$
$= £75.58$

We can of course explain the process involved in rather more detail.

- After 1 year the **simple interest** will be $(60 \times 8 \times 1) \div 100$ = £4.80, which is added to the account.

- So the second year starts with a total amount of £64.80

- At the end of the second year the simple interest will be $(64.80 \times 8 \times 1) \div 100$ = £5.184, which would be rounded off to £5.18 and added to the £64.80 to give a new total amount of £69.98

- At the end of the third year the simple interest will be $(69.98 \times 8 \times 1) \div 100$ = £5.5984, which would be rounded off to £5.60 which, when added to £69.98, will give a final figure of £75.58

Exam Question
During the first few weeks of its life, an octopus increases its body weight by 5% each day. The octopus was born with a body weight of 150 grams. How much will it weigh after:

(a) 1 day?
(b) 3 days?

(NEAB; I)

Solution
(a) It will weigh 150×1.05 = 157.5 g
(b) The quickest solution is to calculate $150 \times (1.05)^3$, which is 173.6438 g. A sensible rounding off would be 174 g.

CONE

A cone is a three-dimensional shape with a circle at the base and a smooth curved surface rising to a point at the top, like a witch's hat.
Where the cone of height h has a base radius r and a slant height l, then:

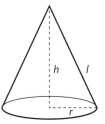

- The *curved surface area* (CSA) is given by the formula CSA = $\pi r l$.

- The *volume* is given by the formula $V = \frac{1}{3}\pi r^2 h$

(This is a Higher Level topic only.)

CONGRUENCE/CONGRUENT

Two shapes are congruent if they are exactly the same shape and size, so that one shape fits exactly on top of the other. This means that the *angles* of one shape are the same as the other shape. It also means that all the *lengths* are the same in one shape as in the other.

Exam Question
State which two shapes in the figure are:

(a) congruent,
(b) **similar** but not congruent.

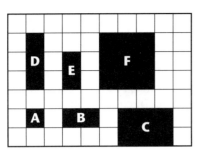

Congruent shapes

Solution
(a) shapes B and E
(b) shapes A and F

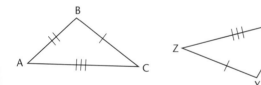
Similar figures

CONGRUENT TRIANGLES

Within the GCSE examination, candidates need to
know whether two *triangles* are congruent or not.
The following examples illustrate the minimum
information needed to determine whether two
triangles are congruent or not:

- In the first pair of triangles, all three sides are the
  same in each triangle, so ABC is congruent to
  XYZ. Usually referred to as SSS (Side, Side, Side).

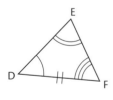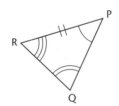

- In the second pair, all three angles and one
  corresponding side are equal, so DEF is congruent
  to PQR. Usually referred to as ASA (Angle, Side,
  Angle).

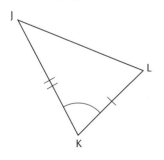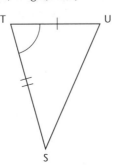

- In the third pair, two sides and the included angle
  are the same, so JKL will be congruent to STU.
  Usually referred to as SAS (Side, Angle, Side).

- In the fourth pair, both are right angled triangles
  with the same length hypotenuse and another of
  the small sides equal. Usually referred to as RHS
  (Right angle, Hypotenuse, Side).

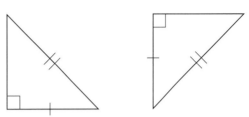

Similar figures

CONSTANTS

Constants are things that do not change. For
instance in $x = 6y - 3$, the 3 is always 3 while the $6y$
will change as y changes. So here the 3 is called the
constant term.

CONSTRUCTIONS

Constructions are where you need to use a pair of
compasses, a pencil and a straight edge, which could
be a ruler if you need to construct precise sizes.
    Notice that you are generally asked to construct
without a protractor. However, you could be asked to
construct a shape containing an awkward angle, such
as 51°, and then you *would* use one.
    The constructions asked within the GCSE will be:

- Line **bisectors**
- Angle **bisectors**
- 60° construction

Specialized constructions

A right angle

To construct a *right angle* at the point D on a line, use
a pair of compasses with an arc of about 4 cm. Then,
with the sharp end on point D, arc each side of point
D to give two marks *equidistant* from D. Next, extend
the arc on the compasses to about 6 or 7 cm. Putting
the sharp end of the compass onto *each of these two
marks in turn*, draw an arc *over* the point D. These
two last arcs should cross over each other, as in the
diagram. Now join up the point D to where these
arcs have crossed and you have your right angle.

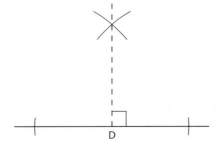

A perpendicular line from a point

We wish to construct the *perpendicular line* from point P to the line AB. Use your compasses to draw as wide an arc as you can cutting AB at two points, with P as the centre of the arc. Then from each point on AB that you have arced, and using the *same* compass opening, make an arc *under* the line AB as shown. The two arcs will cross, giving you the point from which to draw the perpendicular line from P to the line AB.

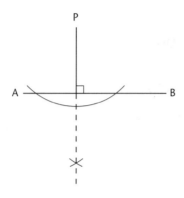

> Remember: Your construction line should always be a faint line.

A 60° angle

To construct a 60° angle at point A on the line AB shown, you can set your compass to any distance you like. Then with the sharp end at point A, draw faintly the quarter circle that arcs through AB. Where this has cut AB, put the sharp end of the compasses (keep it the *same* distance again) and draw the arc faintly that goes from A and cuts through the first arc. Where these two arcs *cross* you can draw a straight line to point A and you have your angle of 60°.

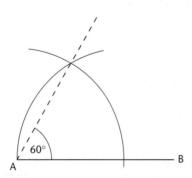

The most common errors in constructions are:

- Not to be accurate enough. Your *measurements* should be correct within 1 mm and your *angles* also should be correct within 1 degree. If you have been asked to construct there is nothing wrong with using your ruler and protractor to *check* what you have done; then if you are inaccurate you can redraw as necessary, provided you have the time.

- To actually use equipment that does not allow you to construct, like set squares and protractors, or even just guessing!

Always *show* all the construction lines so that an examiner can tell that you have constructed. If there are no visible lines of construction, then the examiner will assume that you have used other means and give you no marks at all.

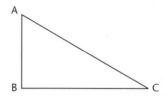

Exam Question

(a) Construct the bisector of angle BAC. Make sure the bisector is drawn long enough to meet BC and label this intersection X.
(b) Measure the lengths of BX and XC, and hence write down the ratio BX:XC.
(c) Show that this ratio is approximately the same ratio as AB:AC.

Solution

(a) You should have bisected the angle using a pair of compasses and *not* a protractor.
(b) Measure the lengths and find their ratio, which should be close to 3:5 or 1:1.6667
(c) You needed to measure the lengths of AB and AC and find their ratio, and you should show this also to be close to 1:1.6667

CHECKPOINT

Can you remember how to:

(a) Construct a line bisector?
(b) Construct an angle bisector?
(c) Construct an angle of 60°?

CONTINUOUS DATA

This is data that *cannot* be measured exactly and is therefore given to some rounded off amount e.g. people's height, weight and age. In every case the measure is suitably rounded off.

When this type of data is used in statistics, its nature has to be recognized when drawing charts or interpreting them.

Discrete data

> Remember: One of the differences between a bar chart and a histogram is that a histogram uses continuous data.

CONVERSION GRAPHS

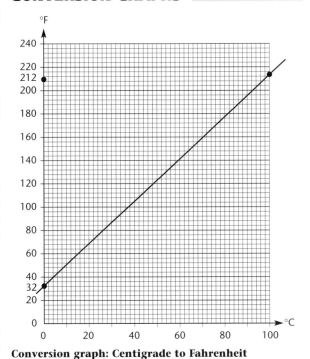

Conversion graph: Centigrade to Fahrenheit

To help *convert* from one unit to another it is often helpful to have a graph which shows the conversion. As an example, a Celsius to Fahrenheit conversion graph is shown. You can find the approximate number of degrees Fahrenheit equal to any number of degrees Celsius, for example, 20 degrees Celsius. From the 20 degrees Celsius mark follow the vertical line up to the graph and then follow it horizontally to approximately 68 degrees Fahrenheit. It can also be worked the other way round to show that 100 degrees Fahrenheit is approximately equal to 38 degrees Celsius.

There are many different types of *conversion graphs*; for instance, from imperial units to metric units, from one currency to another, and so on.

CO-ORDINATES

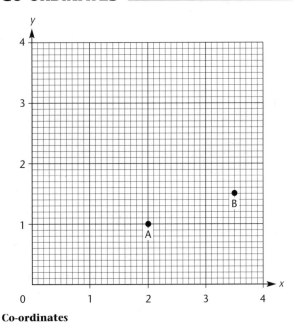

Co-ordinates

Co-ordinates are pairs of numbers that fix a particular position on a grid with reference to some origin.

Cartesian co-ordinates are the usual ones, where the axes used are at right angles to each other. These axes go through the origin and have the numbers marked on them. The *horizontal* axis is usually called the *x*-axis, and the *vertical* one the *y*-axis.

In a pair of co-ordinates we place the number representing the horizontal axis *before* that representing the vertical axis. In the example shown:

● The origin in the diagram is the co-ordinate (0,0).

● The co-ordinates of point A are (2,1).

● The co-ordinates of point B are (3.5, 1.5).

The most common mistake made with co-ordinates is to plot them the wrong way round. Another is to plot them more than 1 mm away from where they should be plotted.

COSINE

Cosine is part of the topic **trigonometry**, and is usually abbreviated to cos. Every angle has a cosine. When the angle is in a *right-angled* triangle, the cosine can be calculated by dividing the side adjacent by the hypotenuse.

$$\cos x = \frac{\text{side adjacent}}{\text{hypotenuse}}$$

Cosine curve

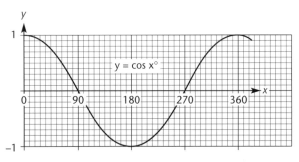

Cosine curve

The curve shown is part of the cosine curve. It will carry on like this for angles greater than 360° and less than 0°. But at the GCSE level you only need to be familiar with the curve between 0° and 360°. Note how *symmetrical* the curve is, and that its height varies between 1 and –1.

> Remember: You use cosine when your situation has two sides making the angle 'cosy'

Cosine rule (Higher Level only)

This can be used to find a missing length or angle in a triangle (*not* a right-angled triangle):

● If all three sides are known, as shown in the first diagram, then any missing angle can be found.

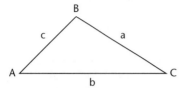

Cosine rule

Where the three sides *a*, *b* and *c* are known, then use the cosine rule as:

$$\cos A = \frac{b^2 + c^2 - a^2}{2bc}$$

$$or \quad \cos B = \frac{a^2 + c^2 - b^2}{2ac}$$

$$or \quad \cos C = \frac{a^2 + b^2 - c^2}{2ab}$$

● If two sides and the included angle are known (as in the second diagram), then the missing side can be found.

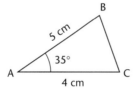

Cosine rule

When the sides *b* and *c* are known, together with the angle A between them, then the cosine rule is:

$$a = \sqrt{(b^2 + c^2 - 2bc \cos A)}$$
$$or \quad b = \sqrt{(a^2 + c^2 - 2ac \cos B)}$$
$$or \quad c = \sqrt{(a^2 + b^2 - 2ab \cos C)}$$

CHECKPOINT

(a) Write down the cosine of 25°.
(b) What angle has a cosine of 0.666?
(c) Find the length BC in the triangle above.

CROSS SECTION

The cross section is the plane shape revealed by cutting a solid shape at right angles to its length (or height). Any shape that has the same cross section throughout its length (or height) is a **prism**.

CUBE

A cube is a three-dimensional shape with six square faces at right angles to each other.
But the term, *cube*, has other meanings:

● To *cube* is to multiply the same number by itself *twice*. For example the cube of 2 is $2 \times 2 \times 2$, which is 8. The *volume of a cube* is found by cubing the length of any edge.

● The *cube root* of a number, say *P*, is that number which, when multiplied by itself twice, gives the number *P*. For example, the cube root of 27 is 3, since $3 \times 3 \times 3 = 27$. The shorthand for cube root is $\sqrt[3]{}$.

CUBIC EQUATION

A cubic equation is one which has a cube as the highest power, e.g:

$$x^3 + 2x^2 - 5 = 0$$

These are solved by graph or trial and improvement.

CUBOID

A cuboid is a three-dimensional shape that has each pair of opposite faces congruent and adjacent faces at right angles to each other. It is also often called a *rectangular block*. Its volume is found by multiplying length by width by height.

CUMULATIVE FREQUENCY

This is sometimes known as a *running total*. It can be quite useful to show the spread of data and to find the **quartiles** of a distribution.
For example, the number of passengers carried on the buses on one particular route during one week was summarized as shown in the table.

Cumulative frequency		
Number of passengers	*Frequency*	*Cumulative frequency*
less than 10	12	12
11–20	23	35
21–30	28	63
31–40	28	91
41–50	9	100

A cumulative frequency diagram is found by plotting the upper class limit with the cumulative frequency.
When we draw the cumulative frequency diagram. We have two choices; either to draw a cumulative frequency polygon which is joining up points with straight lines or a cumulative frequency curve (as shown). Notice the distinctive shape of the *cumulative frequency curve*; it is known as the **ogive** (in a dictionary 'ogive' means 'diagonal'). It can be used to find the **median** and the **quartiles**.

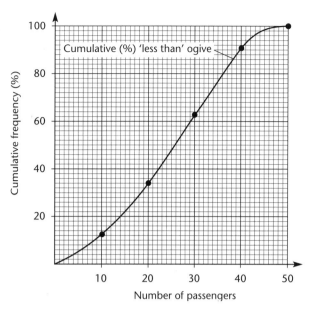

Cumulative frequency (%)

Cumulative (%) 'less than' ogive

Number of passengers

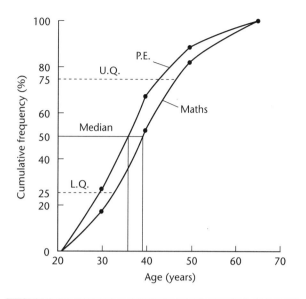

Cumulative frequency (%)

P.E.

U.Q.

Maths

Median

L.Q.

Age (years)

Exam Question

The information in the table shows the percentage distributions by age of teachers of mathematics and physical education in schools in 1996.

	Aged under 30	Aged 30–39	Aged 40–49	Aged 50 and over
Mathematics	17	36	29	18
Physical education	28	39	21	12

(a) Using the same axes and scales, draw cumulative frequency diagrams to represent this information. (You can assume that there were no teachers aged under 21 or aged 65 and over.)

(b) Estimate the difference between the median age of the mathematics teachers and the median age of the physical education teachers.

(c) Estimate the interquartile range for each distribution.

(d) What do you notice about your answers to parts (b) and (c)?

(e) Given that there were 47,900 mathematics teachers, estimate the number aged 45 and over.

(NEAB; I)

Solution

(a) See the diagram with two graphs drawn on it. You can either use a curve or a polygon.

(b) Median maths = 39
median PE = 35

(c) IQ = UQ – LQ
where IQ = interquartile range
UQ = upper quartile
LQ = lower quartile
maths IQ = 45 – 32 = 13
PE IQ = 42 – 29 = 13

(d) Although the medians are different, the interquartile ranges are the same.

(e) 45 is the upper quartile (UQ); hence the number above this age will be one quarter of 47,900, which is 11,975. An approximation at 12,000 would be a good number to use here.

CHECKPOINT

(a) How do you find the interquartile range?

(b) What percentage of the sample is covered by the interquartile range?

CYLINDER

A cylinder is a three-dimensional shape like a drainpipe or a cocoa tin. It is a **prism** with a regular cross section the shape of a circle.

The *volume* of a cylinder is found by multiplying its base area to its height, i.e. volume = $\pi r^2 h$.

The *curved surface area* (that is, just the curved part of the cylinder) is found by multiplying the circumference of the base to its height, i.e. curved surface area = πDh (where D is diameter, = $2r$).

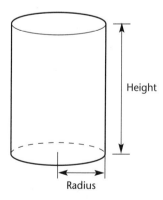

Height

Radius

Cylinder

Exam Question

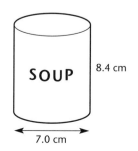

SOUP

8.4 cm

7.0 cm

A cylindrical tin of soup is 8.4 cm tall and has a base diameter of 7.0 cm.

(a) Calculate the area of the base of the tin.

(b) Calculate the capacity of the tin.

Solution

(a) $\pi \times 3.5^2 = 38.48$ cm^2

(b) $38.48451 \times 8.4 = 323$ cm^2

(note we used the accurate value of the base area, then rounded off the answer to 3 s.f.)

DATA

Data is information available for use. There are a number of different types of data that you could come across.

Discrete data

This is data that can be identified on its own by a *single number*. For example, the number of goals scored by various teams, the number of children in a family or the number of records in a teenager's collection.

Continuous data

This is data that *cannot* be measured exactly, and so is given to a rounded off amount. For example, a length of time or the height of trees.

Grouped data

Often we are given non-precise information. This is the case in the table shown below, where a survey was carried out to find the average weight of a class of children. The data has been recorded to the nearest kg and put into the groups as shown.

Weight	Frequency
40–50	3
51–60	14
61–70	8
71–80	1

It is an essential feature of a grouped frequency table such as this that we know what the group boundaries are. Here, for example, the first group will take in weights from 40 kg to 50.4999 (note that the 50.5 would be **rounded** off to 51 and hence be in the higher group). But in the table it is more convenient to show the weights in the way we have done here.

Care has to be taken so that there is no confusion at group boundaries. For example, if we had groups of 40–50, 50–60, 60–70 etc., then it would not be clear what happens at 50 or 60, etc., so this type of grouping must be avoided.

Use is often made of inequalities in grouped frequency. For example:

Weight	Frequency
$40 \leqslant \underline{w} \leqslant 50$	3
$50 < \underline{w} \leqslant 60$	14
$60 < \underline{w} \leqslant 70$	8
$70 < \underline{w} \leqslant 80$	1

This shows a group where every number between 40 and 80 has a place.

Data collection sheet

If you need to simply collect some data to do some analysis on then you want to design a simple data capture sheet. For example:

'Where do you want to go to for the Y11 trip at Easter? Whitby, Alton Towers, or London?'

You can ask a lot of Y11 one day and put the results straight onto a data capture sheet as below:

Where do you want to go?		
Whitby	𝍠𝍠 𝍠𝍠 𝍠𝍠 𝍠𝍠 𝍠𝍠 𝍠𝍠 𝍠𝍠 𝍠𝍠 𝍠𝍠 𝍠𝍠 𝍠𝍠 //	52
Alton Towers	𝍠𝍠 𝍠𝍠 𝍠𝍠 𝍠𝍠 𝍠𝍠 𝍠𝍠 𝍠𝍠 ////	39
London	𝍠𝍠 𝍠𝍠 𝍠𝍠 /	16

Notice how we made space for **tally** marks, and note how we gate the tallies to give groups of fives which makes it easier to count up once the survey is complete.

This is a good data collection sheet: each person asked can easily be given a tally on the sheet and then on to the next person; also, we are concerned with only one question 'where do you want to go?' and we have a list of possible answers on the sheet.

Notice too that since the original question gave specific places we must use those on our data collection sheet. We would lose many marks in the exam if we just asked the open question 'where do you want to go to?'

DECAGON

A ten-sided *polygon*.
The sum of its interior angles is $180 \times 8 = 1440°$. A regular decagon will have 10 lines of symmetry and rotational symmetry of order 10.

the exterior angle is $360 \div 10 = 36°$
the interior angle is $180 - 36 = 144°$

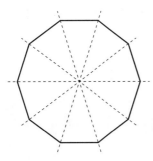

✦ **Polygon**

DECIMAL PLACES

Decimal places are to the right of the decimal point. So the number 4.782 has three decimal places. The table illustrates how **rounding** off is applied to decimal places.

Many mistakes are made in examination answer papers in rounding off decimal places.

Decimal places			
Number	*1*	*2*	*3*
14.5638	14.6	14.56	14.564
0.8572	0.9	0.86	0.857
0.0295	0.0	0.03	0.030

> *Remember: When rounding to 1 decimal place, you look at the 2nd decimal place figure, 5 or more you round up, less than 5 you round down.*

DECIMALS

A decimal is the name used to describe a number with a *decimal point* in it. This decimal point separates the whole numbers from the decimal fractions.

Recurring decimals

Some decimal numbers go on and on, following a particular pattern. For example 0.3333333...; we would call this 0.3 *recurring* or use the mathematical notation '0.3̇'. Some recurring decimals have more than one digit in the repeated pattern, e.g. 0.191919...; this would be represented as '0.1̇9̇'.

There are a number of well-known vulgar fractions that have recurring decimals as their equivalents. The way to find the decimal from a vulgar fraction is to divide the top number by the bottom number. Try this out with fractions like $\frac{1}{11}$, or $\frac{4}{9}$ or even $\frac{2}{7}$.

Terminating decimals

Any decimal number that actually *stops* at so many decimal places is called a *terminating decimal*. For

example $\frac{1}{4}$ will stop at 0.25 and $\frac{3}{8}$ will stop at 0.375; these are just two examples of terminating decimals.

DENSITY

This is a rate, it is the mass per unit volume. The units are usually given as grams per cm^3 (or kilograms per cm^3).

Density is related to mass (weight) and volume, as shown by the following:

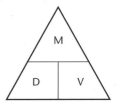

The diagram illustrates that:

$$\text{density} = \frac{\text{mass}}{\text{volume}} \qquad \text{volume} = \frac{\text{mass}}{\text{density}}$$

$$\text{mass} = \text{volume} \times \text{density}$$

Beware – density is defined in terms of mass, which is most commonly referred to as weight. Yes, there is a difference between mass and weight which you learn about in science, but in mathematics questions you will usually be given weight and not mass.

So, be prepared to interchange weight for mass within this topic in mathematics.

Example 1
What is the density of a bar of soap that weights 160 g and has a volume of 95 cm^3?

Solution
$$\text{density} = \frac{\text{mass}}{\text{volume}} = \frac{160 \text{ grams}}{95 \text{ cm}^3} = 1.68 \text{ grams per cm}^3$$

Example 2
What is the weight of 55 cm^3 of a plastic with a density of 0.89 grams/cm^3?

Solution
$$\text{weight (mass)} = \text{volume} \times \text{density}$$
$$= 55 \times 0.89 = 48.95 \text{ grams}$$

Example 3
Find the volume of a substance with density of 1.7 g/cm^3, weighing 300 grams.

Solution
$$\text{volume} = \frac{\text{mass}}{\text{density}} = \frac{300}{1.7} = 176 \text{ cm}^3 \text{ (rounded)}.$$

> *Remember: Be careful with the units, as we have been in the above examples.*

Exam Questions
1. A full skip holds 23 m^3 if filled level with the top. If this skip is filled with earth of density 675 kg/m^3, what is the weight of the earth in the skip?

2. A marble has weight of 0.14 pounds.
1 kg = 2.2 pounds

   (a) Calculate the weight of the marble in grams.
   (b) If the marble has a volume of 1.8 cm³, calculate the density of the marble.

Solutions
1. Use the triangle diagram, which reminds us that weight (mass) = density × volume
$$= 675 \times 23 = 15{,}525 \text{ kg}$$
2. (a) 1,000 grams = 2.2 pounds
$$\frac{1{,}000}{2.2} \text{ grams} = 1 \text{ pound} = 455 \text{ grams}$$
so 0.14 pound = 0.14 × 455 = 63.7 grams
   (b) density = $\dfrac{\text{mass (weight)}}{\text{volume}} = \dfrac{63.7}{1.8} = 35.4 \text{ g/cm}^3$.

CHECKPOINT

How can the fact that

'Mad Dogs are Vicious'

help you remember density rules?

DEPENDENT VARIABLE

✦ *Variable*

DEPOSIT

A deposit is the initial payment made on a hire – purchase agreement. For example, a TV priced at £450 was offered on terms which include a deposit of £45 and a further 12 payments of £40.

The deposit is the first payment made. Usually it is the payment that has to be made before you can take the goods away with you.

DEPRESSION

The depression is the angle made with the horizontal while looking down. It is shown as angle A here.

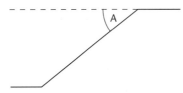

Depression

DIAGONAL

A diagonal is a straight line that joins any two corners of a plane geometric shape.

DIAMETER

A straight line drawn from one side of the circumference of a circle to the other side, passing through the centre, is called a diameter. Any circle will have millions of diameters, all of the same length.

> Remember: The diameter is twice the radius.

DICE

Dice are regular three-dimensional shapes, **polyhedrons**, with numbers on them. The most common sort, and certainly the type meant in any examination question (unless otherwise stated), is the six-sided cube with the numbers 1 to 6. These numbers are linked in such a way that the opposite faces add up to 7 each time.

A single dice is sometimes referred to as a *die*.

DIE

✦ *Dice*

DIMENSIONS

Length

When we have an unknown length in a problem, we represent it by a single letter, followed by the *dimension*, i.e. the unit in which it is measured. For example:

   m centimetres
   y miles
   d kilometres

Example
Find the perimeters of these shapes

(i)   (ii)

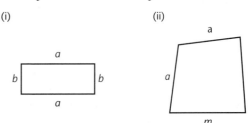

Solution
Shape (i) is a rectangle. Its perimeter is
$$P = a + b + a + b = 2a + 2b$$

Shape (ii) is irregular. Its perimeter is
$$P = a + a + t + m = 2a + t + m$$

Each letter is a length and has a given dimension or measure of length, i.e. centimetre, metre, mile etc. The numbers (coefficients) written before the letters are *not* lengths and therefore have *no* dimension. So for example $2a$, $\frac{1}{2}m$ or $5w$ has the same dimension as a, m or w.

When just one length is involved in a calculation or formula, the calculation or formula is said to have *one dimension* or *1D*, which can be represented by the symbol [L].

Area

Look at these four examples of formulae for calculating area.

$A = ab$ gives the area of a rectangle
$A = a^2$ gives the area of a square
$A = 2ab + 2ac + 2bc$ gives the surface area of a cuboid
$A = \pi r^2$ gives the area of a circle

These formulae have one thing in common. They all consist of terms that are the product of *two* lengths. We can recognize this by counting the number of letters in each term of the formula. The first formula has two (*a* and *b*), the second has two (*a* and *a*). The third has three terms, each of two letters (*a* and *b*, *a* and *c*, *b* and *c*). The fourth also only has two (*r* and *r*) because π is a number (3.14159...), which has no dimension.

Hence we can recognize formulae for area because they only have terms that consist of two letters. That is two lengths multiplied together. They therefore have *two dimensions* or *2D*, which can be represented by the symbol [L × L] or [L²]. Here, again, numbers are not defined as lengths and have no dimension.

This illustrates the units in which area is usually measured. For example, square metres (m × m or m²), square centimetres (cm × cm or cm²).

Volume

Look at these three examples of formulae for calculating volume:

$V = abc$ gives the volume of a cuboid
$V = a^3$ gives the volume of a cube
$V = \pi r^2 h + \frac{3}{4}\pi r^3$ gives the volume of a cylinder with hemispherical ends

Again these formulae have one thing in common. They all consist of terms that are the product of *three* lengths. We recognize this by counting the number of letters in each term of the formula. The first formula has three (*a*, *b* and *c*), the second has three (*a*, *a* and *a*), the third has two terms, each of three letters (*r*, *r*, *h* and *r*, *r*, *r*). Remember π has no dimension.

Hence we can recognize formulae for volume because they only have terms that consist of three letters. That is, three lengths multiplied together. They therefore have *three dimensions* or *3D*, which can be represented by the symbol [L × L × L] or [L³]. Once more, numbers not defined as lengths have no dimension.

This illustrates the units in which volume is usually measured. For example:

cubic metres (m × m × m or m³)
cubic centimetres (cm × cm × cm or cm³)

Consistency

One way in which scientists and mathematicians check complicated formulae to see whether they are correct is to test for *consistency*. That is, to check that every term of the formula is of the same dimension and represents the same *units*. We are only concerned with lengths, areas and volumes, so it is easy for us to test for consistency.

Each term in a formula must have the correct number of dimensions. It is not possible to have a formula with a mixture of terms, some of which have, for example, one dimension and some two dimensions. When terms are found to be mixed, the formula is said to be *inconsistent* and can be rejected.

Example
(a) Which of these formulae are consistent, assuming that each letter represents a length?
(b) If they are consistent, do they represent a length, an area or a volume?

(i) $ab + c$
(ii) $\pi r^2 + ah$
(iii) $p(q + r)$
(iv) $\pi(a^2 + b^2)/h$

Solution
Formula (i) is inconsistent because the first term has two letters (2D) and the second has one letters (1D). Hence, it is a mixture of area and length so it has no meaning, i.e. [L²] + [L] is not possible.

Formula (ii) is consistent because the first term has two letters (*r* and *r*) multiplied by a number (π) and the second term also has two letters (*a* and *h*). Hence, the formula could represent an area, i.e. [L²] + [L²] = [L²] is true.

Formula (iii) is consistent. If we multiply the bracket out, it produces two terms of order 2. Because the bracket is consistent, the whole expression must be. It could represent an area, i.e. [L] × [L] = [L²] is true.

Formula (iv) is also consistent. There are two 2D terms on the top line and one 1D term on the bottom. One dimension can be cancelled to give two terms of order 1. Hence the formula represents a length. i.e. [L²] ÷ [L] = [L] is true.

Exam Question
Taking *l*, *b*, *h* and *r* to be lengths, complete the table to show which of the formulae 1, 2, 3, 4 or 5 denotes length, area or volume.

	Formula
Length	
Area	
Volume	

Formulae:
1. $h^2(r + b)$
2. $\pi r(l + b)$
3. $4\,h \times b$
4. $\pi\sqrt{(h^2 - b^2)}$
5. $b^2\left(\dfrac{h}{3} + r\right)$

Solution

	Formula
Length	4
Area	2, 3
Volume	1, 5

DIRECTED NUMBERS

Directed numbers is a term sometimes used to describe positive and negative arithmetic. Look at the number line shown, and you will see a scale rather like that on a thermometer. There is a 0; then above the zero are positive numbers and below the zero are negative numbers. The negative numbers are also called *minus* numbers; for example 3 below the zero is usually referred to as minus 3, but written as –3.

Adding and subtracting

There are a set of rules that you ought to know:

+ – is the same as –
– – is the same as +

So you see that:

- 4 + –3 is the same as 4 – 3, which is 1
- 4 – –3 is the same as 4 + 3, which is 7

For example:

2 + 6 = 8	2 – 6 = –4
2 – –6 = 8	2 + –6 = –4
–2 + 6 = 4	–2 – 6 = –8
–2 – –6 = 4	–2 + –6 = –8

$$\begin{array}{c} 5 \\ 4 \\ 3 \\ 2 \\ 1 \\ 0 \\ -1 \\ -2 \\ -3 \end{array}$$

Multiplying and dividing

There are a set of rules that you ought to know:

+ × + = +
– × – = +   *Signs the same answer*: **+**

+ × – = –
– × + = –   *Signs different answer*: **–**

An easy way to remember these rules is that when the *signs are the same* the answer is a *positive*, and when the *signs are different* then the answer is *negative*.

For example:

2 × 3 = 6	2 × –3 = –6
–2 × –3 = 6	–2 × 3 = –6
6 ÷ 3 = 2	6 ÷ –3 = –2
–6 ÷ –3 = 2	–6 ÷ 3 = –2

Many errors are made by candidates in this kind of arithmetic. These are mainly careless errors of getting the signs wrong, so do learn the rules.

Exam Question
(a) How many degrees colder is Londonderry at 6 a.m. than at midday?

(b) The temperature in Omagh rises by 6 °C between 6 a.m. and midday.
    Give the temperature at midday.

(NISEAC; F)

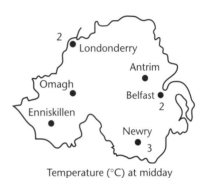

Temperature (°C) at 6 a.m.

Temperature (°C) at midday

Solution
(a) 2 – –5 = 7 °C
(b) –2 + 6 = 4 °C

DISCOUNT

A discount is a deduction from the usual amount paid. Often people are given a discount for paying cash for their goods or for being an employee or a member of a particular union. This discount is usually a *percentage*, and always a percentage *reduction*. For example:

James as a paper boy in a newsagent's shop is allowed 5% discount on any goods bought over £1. How much will he pay for a game priced at £7.60?

The 5% discount on £7.60 will be $7.60 \times \frac{5}{100} = £0.38$
So James will pay £7.60 – £0.38 = £7.22

DISCRETE DATA

Discrete data is data that can be identified on its own by a single number. For example, the number of teeth you have or the number of televisions in your home.

✥ *Data*

DIVIDING/DIVISION

✥ *Directed numbers*

The symbol for dividing is usually ÷, but the use of a fraction notation also means divide, e.g. 3/5, meaning 3 divided by 5.

The most difficult division can be done by using your calculator and perhaps rounding off the answer. But you do need to be able to do division without a calculator. This will fall into the two types, simple and long.

Simple division

For example: 780 ÷ 4. There are quite a few ways to do this, one of which is set out like this:

```
    195
4 )780
    38
    20
```

- We divide the 4 into the 7 first to get 1 remainder 3, the 3 being put next to the 8 to give 38.

- Next we divide 4 into the 38 to give 9 remainder 2, the 2 being put next to the 0 to make 20.

- Finally, we divide the 20 by 4 to give 5.

- So the solution will be 780 ÷ 4 = 195

Long division

This involves dividing a number bigger than 10. Example: 395 ÷ 17. There are many different ways to do this, but the traditional way is to do the following:

```
     23
17 )395
     34
     55
     51
      4
```

- We set out the problem carefully and first ask, how many 17s in 39? We can work out it must be 2.

- So we multiply 17 by 2 putting the answer 34 under the 39.

- Now take 34 away from 39 and bring down the 5 to give 55.

- Now, how many 17s in 55? We can see it to be 3.

- Multiply 17 by 3 to get 51, put this under the 55 and take away.

- We get 4 which is the remainder since there is nothing left to bring down.

- Hence the answer is 395 ÷ 17 = 23 remainder 4.

Look out for the signs in your exam about not using a calculator and showing how you did your division without a calculator.

DRAWING

The type of drawing referred to in a GCSE mathematics syllabus is geometrical drawing. The main objective in drawing diagrams accurately or to scale is to convey information.

You need to be able to use a protractor, a pair of compasses, a set square and, of course, a ruler. When asked to draw a diagram (or to **construct** it) the usual accuracy looked for is to be no more than 1 or 2 degrees out on the angles, and less than 1 mm out on the lengths. Being inaccurate is the most common error made while drawing in mathematics.

EDGE

An edge is found on three-dimensional shapes where two faces meet.

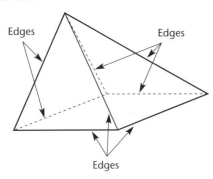

Edge

ELEVATION

In GCSE mathematics you need to be aware of the different aspects of elevation.

Angle of elevation

The angle of elevation is the angle made with the horizontal while looking up, as shown below.

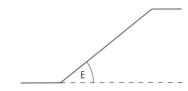

Angle of elevation

End elevation

The end elevation of a shape is the view you get when looking at the end of a shape. For example, in

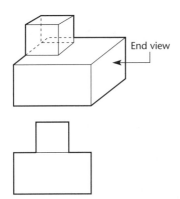

End elevation

the shape shown, the end elevation is found by looking in the direction of the arrow. The end elevation is drawn underneath the shape.

Front elevation

The front elevation of a shape is the view you get when you look directly at the front of a shape. For example, in the shape shown, the front elevation is found by looking in the direction of the arrow. The front elevation is drawn underneath the shape.

The most common errors are to draw an elevation with **perspective**, that is to try and make it look like a three-dimensional drawing instead of a plane diagram in two dimensions only.

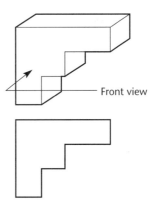

Front elevation

ENLARGEMENT

When all the respective dimensions of two shapes are in the *same ratio*, then each shape is an enlargement of the other.

Geometric enlargement

The idea of an enlargement is to make a shape of different size (usually larger but it could be smaller), and in a specific place:

- You will be given a *scale factor* which tells you how many times bigger each line will be.

- You will also be given a *centre of enlargement* which will determine *where* the enlargement ends up.

For example, to enlarge the shaded shape shown with a scale factor of two from the centre of enlargement X, the distance from the centre of

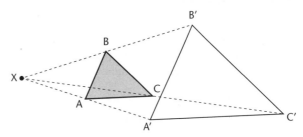

Geometric enlargement

enlargement to each vertex in the shape is multiplied by two. This is shown in the diagram by the dotted lines. The enlarged shape will have all its dimensions multiplied by the scale factor, but will keep all angles the same. In other words, the two shapes will be **similar** shapes.

> Remember: In an enlargement, every length is enlarged by the scale factor, so that new length = original length × scale factor.

Negative enlargement

When asked to draw an enlargement with a negative scale factor, then you need to draw the lines back through the centre of enlargement (the opposite way round to a positive scale factor that we described above). Then enlarge as before.

* The shaded triangle has been enlarged with a scale factor of –2 with * as the centre of enlargement. The enlarged shape under negative enlargement will always end *upside down*, but will still be a **similar** shape to the original.

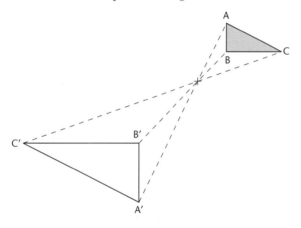

EQUATIONS

Equations are mathematical statements that one expression is equal to another. In other words two (or more) quantities are joined by an equal sign. For example, $4x + 2 = 2x + 10$ is an equation.

The *solution* of an equation refers to the value (or values) of the variable (here x) which make the equals sign hold true. Our solution in this case is $x = 4$ At any other value of the variable, x, the equality sign does not hold true.

Types of equation

There are many different types of equation that you will come across in GCSE. You will often be asked to find a solution to these equations, that is, the numbers that make both sides equal.

Linear equations

Linear equations involve single variables of power 1. They contain no expressions such as x^2, x^3, $\frac{1}{x}$, xy etc. For example:

$$x + y = 6 \quad 5x - 3 = 2y \quad 3(x - 2) = (2x - 1)$$

These can usually be solved by moving the equation around using the well-known phrase – 'If it's doing what it's doing to the rest of that side then you can move it from one side of the equation to the other and make it do the opposite job.'

Exam Question
Solve the equation $3 (x - 2) = 5 (x + 3)$

Solution
$$3x - 6 = 5x + 15$$
$$3x - 5x = 15 + 6$$
$$-2x = 21$$
$$x = \frac{21}{-2} = -10.5$$

Quadratic equations

A quadratic equation is an equation involving a variable with the power 2, e.g:

$$x^2 + 5x + 6 = 0$$

Here the highest power is a two. To solve quadratic equations you can use one of three methods:

1. *Factorize*
   Quadratic factorization is where we put the quadratic back into two brackets and solve those brackets.
   For example, solve $x^2 + x - 12 = 0$

   Factorizing into two brackets gives us
   $(x + 4) (x - 3) = 0$
   Hence $(x + 4) = 0$ or $(x - 3) = 0$
   hence $x = -4$ or $x = 3$.
   The solution is $x = -4$ and 3.

2. *Formula*
   You can solve a **quadratic** equation of the form $ax^2 + bx + c = 0$ by the formula:

   $$x = \frac{-b \pm \sqrt{b^2 - 4ac}}{2a}$$

   For example, solve $2x^2 + 5x - 3 = 0$
   Use the formula where $a = 2$, $b = 5$, $c = -3$

   $$\text{then } x = \frac{-5 \pm \sqrt{25 - -24}}{4}$$

   $$x = \frac{-5 \pm \sqrt{49}}{4}$$

   $$\text{then } x = \frac{-5 \pm 7}{4}$$

   $$\text{Hence } x = \frac{-12}{4} \text{ and } \frac{2}{4}$$
   $$= -3 \text{ and } 0.5$$

3. *Completing the square*
   You can solve any **quadratic** equation by making a square and rooting.
   For example, solve $x^2 - 8x + 12 = 0$

   Find a square as near as possible that fits the left-hand side. For instance $(x - 4)^2$ which is $x^2 - 8x + 16$.

Our equation can now be rewritten as:

$$x^2 - 8x + 16 = 16 - 12 = 4$$
$$(x - 4)^2 = 4$$
$$(x - 4) = 2 \text{ or } -2$$

Hence $x = 2 + 4 = 6$ or $x = -2 + 4 = 2$
    So $x = 6$ and 2

Any of the above methods can be used to solve your quadratic equation, but do use the method that you are familiar with and are confident about using.

✛ *Factorization, Formula, Quadratic, Variables*

Fractional equations

Fractional equations of the type $\frac{x}{3} + \frac{x-2}{4} = 2$ can be solved by changing both fractions to *equivalent fractions* with the same bottom number (denominator). Then carry on using normal algebraic techniques.

    For example, solve the following equation:

$$\frac{x}{3} + \frac{x-2}{4} = 3$$

Change both fractions to a 12 on the bottom hence:

$$\frac{4x}{12} + \frac{3x-6}{12} = 3$$

$$4x + 3x - 6 = 36$$
$$7x = 42$$
$$x = 6$$

Simultaneous equations

Simultaneous equations are where two equations both need solving at the same time. These equations are usually linear but not necessarily so, and one could well be quadratic. There are two common methods for solving simultaneous equations:

1. *Substitution method*
    The technique is to *substitute* one equation into the other and so eliminate one of the variables. Then solve for the variable left and substitute back to find the value of the eliminated variable.
    For example, solve: $x + 2y = 13$ . . . . (i)
    $\qquad\qquad\qquad\quad 4x - y = 7$ . . . . . (ii)

Substitute (i) ($x = 13 - 2y$) into (ii) to give
$4(13 - 2y) - y = 7$
Now we only have one unknown variable, y, and one equation.

$$52 - 8y - y = 7$$
$$52 - 7 = 9y$$
$$\text{Hence } 45 = 9y$$
$$\text{So} \qquad y = 5$$

Now substitute this back into equation (i) to give us $x + 10 = 13$, so $x = 3$. The solution of the simultaneous equations is $x = 3$ and $y = 5$

2. *Elimination method*
    The technique is to *eliminate* one variable by adding or subtracting the two equations. Then proceed as above.
    For example, solve $3x - y = 9$ . . . . . (i)
    $\qquad\qquad\qquad\quad 5x + y = 23$ . . . . (ii)

Add (i) to (ii) to eliminate y, then $8x = 32$, hence $x = 4$.
Substituting into (i), then $12 - y = 9$, and $3 = y$.
So the solution of the simultaneous equation is $x = 4$ and $y = 3$.

The most common error to be made here by candidates in examinations is not to check their answers. A simple and effective technique is to check that your solution works by substituting it into the equation you did not substitute into before. Doing this at least allows you a check to see if you could be wrong. If you are, then you can have another go if you have time.

Exam Question
Solve the simultaneous equations:
$$4x - y = 3 \text{ . . . . . (i)}$$
$$3x + 2y = 16 \text{ . . . . (ii)}$$

(Intermediate)

Solution
Here we use the *elimination* method, though the substitution method would be equally acceptable.
    To eliminate y we need to double the whole of equation (i) to give

$$8x - 2y = 6$$
$$3x + 2y = 16$$

Now we can add the equations to eliminate y, to give $11x = 22$, making $x = 2$, which is substituted into equation (i) – being the simplest – to give $8 - y = 3$, or $y = 5$. So the final solution is $x = 2$, $y = 5$.

CHECKPOINT

Can you solve the:

(a) Linear equation: $5x - 3 = 4$
(b) Quadratic equation: $(x + 2)(x - 3) = 0$
(c) Simultaneous equations: $5x + y = 11$
$\qquad\qquad\qquad\qquad\qquad\quad 3x - y = 5$

✛ *Simultaneous equations*

EQUIVALENT

Two expressions that are equivalent will have the same value but could well appear different.

Equivalent fractions

These are *fractions* that have the same value but which look different. Any two equivalent fractions will have the same decimal fraction and will cancel down to the same *vulgar fraction*.

For example, $\frac{1}{2}, \frac{3}{6}, \frac{6}{12}, \frac{7}{14}, \frac{2}{4}$, etc. are all equivalent fractions that cancel down to 0.5 or $\frac{1}{2}$.

ESTIMATION

An estimation is a calculated guess at some length, weight or other amount. We *estimate* by referring to things we already know. For example, it will help in estimating the weight of a book if we can already recognize a particular weight, like a bag of sugar, which represents 1 kg. We can then ask ourselves whether the book is twice that weight, or the same, or even smaller, etc.

To be good at estimating depends partly on experience and partly on a knowledge of standard weights and measures.

> *Remember: You will estimate the answer to a sum by rounding each number to 1 significant figure, then estimating the result.*

EXCHANGE RATES

Exchange rates			
The pound abroad *(1st April 1998)*			
Austria	Sch 20.83	Hong Kong	HK$ 12.67
Belgium	Fr 61.04	Ireland	1£ 1.17
Canada	C$ 2.34	Italy	L 2,947
Denmark	Kr 11.35	Norway	NKr 12.30
France	Fr 9.90	Spain	Pes 250
Germany	DM 2.96	Switzerland	Fr 2.45
Greece	Drc 516.34	USA	$1.64
Holland	Gld 3.32		

The table shows the exchange rates for the British pound on April 1st, 1998. The table indicates the amount of each foreign currency you would have received for £1 on that day. These rates do change day by day, so any table soon becomes out of date. To exchange *back* into British pounds, you will need another table. This will have different rates since the money exchangers take their cut! So you may well exchange £50 for say 495 French francs, but then if you try to exchange this back into pounds you would probably only get about £45.

EXPAND

To expand within mathematics usually means to multiply out the brackets. For example expand $5(3x + 4y)$, means multiply the bracket by 5 to give $15x + 20y$.

Expand and simplify $(2x + 3)(4x - 1)$ means to multiply out then simplify as:

$$(2x + 3)(4x - 1) = 8x^2 - 2x + 12x - 3$$
$$= 8x^2 + 10x - 3$$

EXPECTATION

This often refers to that part of *probability* where we try to work out the *expectation* of a certain result. This is found out by multiplying the *probability of an event* by the *number of trials* for that event. For example:

A doctor found by random trial that out of 50 of his patients 17 of them had back trouble. How many of his 2,000 patients are likely to suffer back trouble?

The probability of any one patient at random having back trouble is $\frac{17}{50}$

So the *expectation* of the total number of his 2,000 patients having back trouble will be $\frac{17}{50} \times 2,000$, which is 680. So the doctor can expect around 680 of his patients to have back trouble.

EXPONENT

An exponent is the power to which a term has been raised. For example in 10^3 the exponent is 3. You will see this on your scientific calculator in two ways:

1. The E that you sometimes see on the calculator display. For example 4.56 E 9 is the calculator shorthand for *standard form*, where the number is actually 4.56×10^9 or 4,560,000,000.

2. The button that is marked either EXP or E or even EE (check to see which it is) on your calculator. You use this to put a standard form number into the calculator yourself. For example, to put in the standard form number 8.5×10^2, you would key in 8.5 EXP 2. Try it out.

FACE

A face is a surface of a three-dimensional figure bounded by edges. **Edges** are where two faces meet.

FACTOR

The factors of a whole number N are the whole numbers that will divide into N exactly. For example, the factors of 16 are 1, 2, 4, 8 and 16.

Exam Question
(a) List the set of factors of
   (i) 48
   (ii) 72
(b) List the common factors of 48 and 72
(c) (i) List the prime factors of 48
    (ii) Express 48 as a product of primes

(NEAB; F)

Solution
(a) (i) 1, 2, 3, 4, 6, 8, 12, 16, 24 and 48
   (ii) 1, 2, 3, 4, 6, 8, 9, 12, 18, 24, 36 and 72
(b) 1, 2, 3, 4, 6, 8, 12, 24
(c) (i) 2, 3
   (ii) $2^4 \times 3$

Prime factors of a number are the **prime** numbers that will multiply to create the number.

Examples
The prime factors of 12 are $2 \times 2 \times 3$
The prime factors of 36 are $2 \times 2 \times 3 \times 3$

Exam Question
(a) Express 360 as a product of powers of its prime factors.
(b) What is the lowest number which 360 must be multiplied by to become a square number?

Solution
(a) $2 \times 2 \times 2 \times 3 \times 3 \times 5$
(b) We need to create $2 \times 2 \times 2 \times 2 \times 3 \times 3 \times 5 \times 5$
the extra numbers needed are $2 \times 5 = 10$.

⟡ *Prime, Prime factors*

FACTORIZATION/FACTORIZE

To factorize means to separate an expression into the parts that will multiply together to give that expression. The two (or more) parts are usually connected by brackets. For example:

$2p + pt$ can be factorized to give $p (2 + t)$
$5ab - ab^2$ can be factorized to give $ab (5 - b)$

Quadratic factorization

This means putting a **quadratic** expression back into its brackets, if at all possible. It is helpful when factorizing to first consider what the *signs* may be:

● When the last sign in the quadratic $ax^2 + bx + c$ is positive, then both signs in the brackets are the *same* as the *first sign* in the quadratic. For example:

$$x^2 + 5x + 4 = (\quad + \quad)(\quad + \quad)$$
and $\quad x^2 - 5x + 4 = (\quad - \quad)(\quad - \quad)$

● When the last sign in the quadratic $ax^2 + bx - c$ is *negative*, then the signs in the brackets are *different*. For example:

$$x^2 + 5x - 4 = (\quad + \quad)(\quad - \quad)$$

Once you've sorted out the *signs*, then you need to look at the *numbers*. Follow through these two examples to see how to do this

Example 1
Factorize $x^2 + 6x + 8$

By looking at the *signs* we see that the brackets both contain the *same* sign which will be a +. We then see that the *end numbers* in each bracket must multiply together to give 8. This could be 1×8 or 2×4. But the combination must add together to give 6, so this will be the 2×4 combination.

Hence the factorization is $(x + 2)(x + 4)$.

Example 2
Factorize $x^2 + x - 12$

By looking at the signs we can see that both the brackets will have a *different* sign. We then see that the *end numbers* will multiply together to give a 12. This could be 1×12 or 2×6 or 3×4. But the combination must give a difference of 1, so this will be the 3×4 combination. The larger number needs to be positive since the quadratic has $+ x$ in the middle.

Hence the factorization is $(x + 4)(x - 3)$.

Exam Question
1. Factorize completely $6xy^2 - 12x^2y$
2. (a) Expand $(3x + 1)(x - 4)$
   (b) Factorize completely $6x^2 - 8x$

Solution
1. $6xy (y - 2x)$
2. (a) $3x^2 - 12x + x - 4 = 3x^2 - 11x - 4$
   (b) $2x (3x - 4)$

> *Remember: After factorizing, you can check your answer by multiplying out again.*

FINITE

A finite number is a countable number. If a number is too big to be counted, then it is called **infinite**. For example, the number of grains of sand in the world. Although this last example is a fixed number at any one point in time, it is just impossible to count them all since there are so many. So we would use the term infinite in this case.

FORMULA

A formula is a set procedure to follow in order to work something out. It is a general expression that can be applied to several different values of the quantities in question. A formula can be in the form of a flow chart. Sometimes it can be a *sentence*, e.g. 'Wages are calculated by multiplying the number of years worked by £10 and then adding on £45.'

Most commonly, however, a formula is expressed algebraically. For example:

Wages in £s = $10x + 45$, where x = number of years worked.

FRACTION

A fraction is an expression which contains a *part* of a whole. There are two main types of fraction: vulgar fractions and decimal fractions.

Vulgar fractions

A vulgar fraction is expressed using two whole numbers, one above the other. For instance $\frac{3}{5}, \frac{4}{6}, \frac{12}{17}$ and so on.

Decimal fractions

A decimal fraction is one that uses a decimal point and has decimal places to represent tenths, hundredths, thousandths, etc.

Equivalent fractions

Equivalent fractions are fractions that are equal to each other but may well look different. Equivalent vulgar fractions will cancel down to the same vulgar fraction. To find a decimal fraction equivalent to a vulgar fraction, just divide the top number by the bottom number.

In the example $\frac{3}{5}$, the 5 represents a whole unit divided into 5 equal pieces; the 3 represents the use of 3 of these 5 equal pieces. The top number is called the *numerator* and the bottom number is called the *denominator*.

Cancelling fractions

When we can divide *both* the numerator and the denominator by the same number exactly, then we can cancel down.

An example illustrating this is the fraction $\frac{10}{12}$ being cancelled down to $\frac{5}{6}$ by dividing both top and bottom by the same thing, in this case a 2.

Addition and subtraction of fractions

To add or subtract two fractions change them to equivalent fractions with the same bottom number denominator, then add or subtract:

Example 1

$\frac{1}{5} + \frac{2}{3} = \frac{3}{15} + \frac{10}{15} = \frac{13}{15}$

(we use 15 since it is the smallest multiple of both 3 and 5)

Example 2

$\frac{3}{4} - \frac{1}{6} = \frac{9}{12} - \frac{2}{12} = \frac{7}{12}$

(we use 12 since it is the smallest multiple of both 4 and 6)

Multiplication of fractions

To multiply two fractions you simply need to multiply the top two numbers and multiply the bottom two numbers.

Example 3

$\frac{2}{5} \times \frac{3}{8} = \frac{6}{40} = \frac{3}{20}$ (after cancelling down)

Division of fractions

To divide two fractions, you turn the second one upside down and then multiply the two together

Example 4

$\frac{2}{5} \div \frac{3}{4} = \frac{2}{5} \times \frac{4}{3} = \frac{8}{15}$

Exam Question

Mr Dane leaves his home near Sheffield to travel to Birmingham by car. Before he sets off he looks at his petrol gauge and milometer, which are as shown in the figure.

(a) What fraction of a full tank of petrol is shown by the petrol gauge?
(b) Write your answer to part (a) as a decimal.

Later that day Mr Dane arrives back in Sheffield and notices that his petrol tank is now one-quarter full and his milometer reads 35,468.

(c) How many miles has Mr Dane travelled?
(d) What fraction of a full tank of petrol has been used?
(e) Mr Dane spent 4 hours travelling. Calculate his average speed for the journey. Give your answer to the nearest mile per hour.

(NEAB; I)

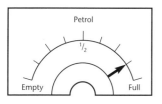

3	5	2	8	9

Miles

Box weight (w)	f.d. × width	Frequency
$0 \leqslant w \leqslant 10$	5×10	= 50
$10 < w \leqslant 20$	30×10	= 300
$20 < w \leqslant 30$	60×10	= 600
$30 < w \leqslant 50$	20×20	= 400
$50 < w \leqslant 60$	10×10	= 100

Solution

(a) $\frac{7}{8}$

(b) 0.875

(c) 35,468 – 35,289 = 179 miles

(d) $\frac{7}{8} - \frac{1}{4} = \frac{7}{8} - \frac{2}{8} = \frac{5}{8}$

(e) 179 ÷ 4 = 44.75
     = 45 m.p.h.

FREQUENCY

Frequency is the number of times some defined event occurs. This can be found by the use of a **tally chart**. Frequency can be represented by the use of **bar charts**, **pictograms**, **pie charts** and **histograms**.

Grouped frequency

✛ **Grouped data** *under the heading* **Data**

Cumulative frequency

Cumulative frequency is sometimes known as *running totals*. They can be most useful in finding **medians** and **quartiles**.

✛ **Cumulative**

Frequency density

This is used as the vertical axis on a **histogram** which has unequal block widths. Frequency density is

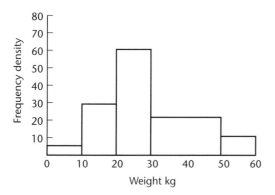

Frequency density

abbreviated as f.d. The frequency that any block represents on a histogram is given by the area of the block. This is found by multiplying the width of the block by its height as given on the frequency density axis.

For example the histogram shown illustrates the number of boxes handled in one particular week by a packaging company. From the histogram we can build up the table to illustrate the *frequency* of each group.

CHECKPOINT

From the frequency chart

Score x	Frequency
$0 < x \leqslant 20$	3
$20 < x \leqslant 40$	9
$40 < x \leqslant 60$	23
$60 < x \leqslant 80$	11
$80 < x \leqslant 100$	4

Explain how you would:

(i) Estimate the mean.
(ii) Estimate the median.

✛ **Average, Cumulative frequency, Histogram, Mean, Median**

FUNCTIONS

A function is a mapping from one set to another where each element in the initial set, called the domain, will map to one, and only one, element in the **image** set (or **range**).

A function is another way of writing an algebraic formula. We generally use the notation of f(x) for the image of x under the function f. For example, where the function $f(x) = 4x + 3$, then $f(2) = 11$, since substituting $x = 2$ into $4x + 3$ gives us 11. In other words, it is another way of writing $y = 4x + 3$ where we talk about f(x) instead of y. Another way of expressing the function f is as $f:x \rightarrow 4x + 3$.

GENERALIZE

To generalize means to find out the pattern in a situation, often a sequence of numbers, and to express this pattern in general terms using algebra.

We usually refer to this as finding the nth term, where n stands for the number of the sequence. The sequences you are likely to meet are linear sequences and quadratic sequences.

To find the nth term of a linear sequence

A linear sequence has the *same differences* between each pair of consecutive terms, e.g.:

4, 7, 10, 13, 16 . . . . difference of 3
5, 9, 13, 17, 21 . . . . difference of 4

The nth term of a linear sequence is always of the form $An + b$, where

- A is the difference between each pair of consecutive terms

- b is the difference between the first term and A

Example 1
Find the nth term of the sequence 4, 7, 10, 13, 16 . . . .

Solution
The difference between consecutive terms is 3. So the first part of the nth term is $3n$. Subtract the difference, 3, from the first term, 4, which gives $4 - 3 = 1$.

So the nth term is given by $3n + 1$.

(You can test it by substituting $n = 1, 2, 3, 4, \ldots$)

Example 2
From the sequence 2, 6, 10, 14, 18 . . . , find:

(a) The nth term
(b) The 50th term

Solution
(a) The difference between consecutive terms is 4, so the first part of the nth term is $4n$.
Subtract 4 from the first term 2, which gives $b = -2$

So the nth term is given by $4n - 2$

(b) The 50th term is found by substituting $n = 50$ into the rule, $4n - 2$

So 50th term $= 4 \times 50 - 2 = 200 - 2$
$= 198$

To find the nth term of a quadratic sequence

Many situations that arise in problem solving can be solved when you find the generalization of the pattern is a quadratic rule.

You should suspect that a pattern is quadratic when you notice the differences keep increasing.

Many patterns are based on n^2, so you do need to recognize the pattern 1, 4, 9, 16, 25. . . . The differences of this pattern are the odd numbers 3, 5, 7, 9 . . ., so if you spot the odd numbers as the differences you know the pattern is based on n^2.

Work through the following examples to see how sequences can be spotted if they are built around n^2.

Example 1
Find the nth term in the sequence:

3, 6, 11, 18, 27 . . .

Solution
We can see the differences are the odd numbers 3, 5, 7, 9 . . . so we know the rule is built around n^2.
Next we look for a link with the square numbers, 1, 4, 9, 16, 25 . . .
It is pretty easy to see the link is the square numbers with 2 added to each term, the nth term is $n^2 + 2$

(You can always do a quick check on the generalization with $n = 1, 2, 3, 4$ to see if it does work.)

Exam Question
Alison often called in at the Rose Cottage Café with friends for a pot of tea. During one summer she noted that:

a pot of tea for 2 people cost 80p
a pot of tea for 3 people cost 95p
a pot of tea for 4 people cost £1.10

(a) What would be the cost of a pot of tea for:
   (i) 5 people?
   (ii) 1 person?
(b) Write down the formula that the Rose Cottage Café uses to calculate the cost of a pot of tea.

(NEAB; F)

Solution
Notice the list goes up 15p each time, hence

(a) (i) £1.10 + 15p = £1.25
   (ii) 80p – 15p = 65p
(b) Cost = 50p + 15n, where n is the number of people,
   or Cost = 65p + 15n, where n is the number of extra people

Exam Question
(a) What is the next number in this sequence.
   1, 3, 7, 13 . . .
(b) Find a formula, in terms of n, for the number of sticks in the nth shape in this sequence.

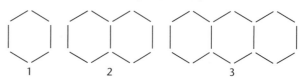

(c) Find a formula, in terms of n, for the nth term in this sequence.
2, 5, 10, 17, 26 . . .

Solution

(a) The differences are 2, 4, 6, 8
So the next number in the sequence will be
13 + 8 = 21

(b) Find the number pattern of the sticks; 6, 11, 16 . . .
the common difference is 5 and the difference between the difference and the first term is 1.
So the nth term will be $5n + 1$

(c) The differences go up in 3, 5, 7, 9 which is the odd numbers, which suggests we look at a number sequence based on the square numbers. It should not be long before you find the sequence $n^2 + 1$.

CHECKPOINT

Write down the nth term of the following sequences:

(a) 4, 11, 18, 25 . . .
(b) 4, 7, 12, 19 . . .

GEOMETRY

Geometry can be defined as the study of solid shapes, surfaces, curves, lines and points in space. There are many geometrical facts to remember, particularly those concerning triangles, polygons and circles.

Transformation geometry

Transformation geometry looks at how shapes change position and size according to certain rules that we call **transformations**. The common transformations at GCSE level are **translations**, **rotations**, **reflections** and **enlargements**.

GRADIENT

The gradient of a line is its *steepness*; the bigger the gradient the steeper it is to go up the hill. A *negative* gradient means going downhill.
To be precise, the gradient of a straight line is the vertical distance divided by the horizontal distance between any two points on that straight line.

Measuring gradients

Gradient on a straight line

In general, if we have a *straight line*, as shown, and choose two points P (x_1, y_1) and Q (x_2, y_2) that both lie on the line, then the gradient is given by

$$\frac{y_2 - y_1}{x_2 - x_1}$$

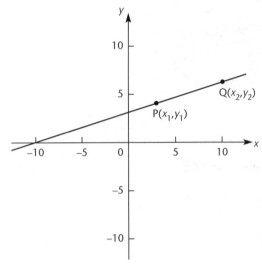

Gradient

This will always automatically get the sign correct, which is + ve uphill and – ve downhill.

Gradient on a curve

To find the gradient on a curve, you must draw a **tangent** to the curve at the point in question. You must then find the gradient of the tangent. Of course the gradient keeps changing on a curve.

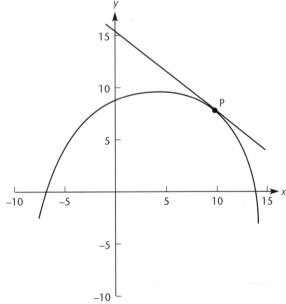

Gradient on a curve

Remember: When finding a gradient the longer the line the more accurate will be your gradient.

Certain gradients are particularly useful and ought to be known. The gradient on a distance/time graph will represent the **speed** or *velocity*. The gradient on a velocity/time graph will represent the **acceleration** (see the accompanying graphs). Negative acceleration is *deceleration*. Notice how the **units** of a gradient come from the units on the axes.

(a)

(b)

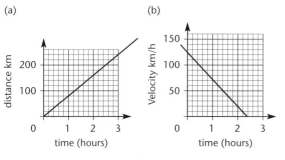

Velocity = $\dfrac{240 \text{ km}}{3 \text{ hrs}}$ = 80 km/h   Acceleration = $\dfrac{-125}{2.4}$ = –52.1 km/h^2

Any **linear** equation of the type $y = mx + c$ has a gradient m, where m is the coefficient of x.

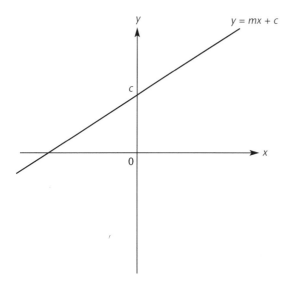

Exam Question

A hill whose gradient is 1 in 5 can be said to have a gradient of 20%. Express a gradient of 1 in 7 as a percentage correct to the nearest integer.

(NEAB; I)

Solution

$\frac{1}{7} \times 100$ = 14% (to the nearest integer)

GRAPHS

A graph is a visual picture of information or data. It is usually in the form of a set of co-ordinates on a cartesian grid, where the axes are perpendicular. **Equations** have graphs to represent the many values that satisfy that equation.

(a)

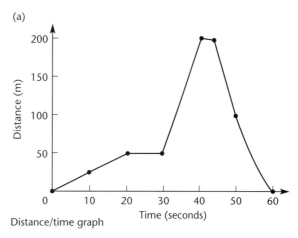

Distance/time graph

(b)

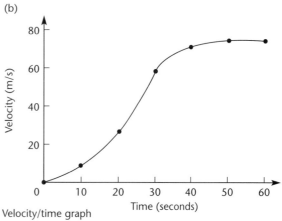

Velocity/time graph

Travel graphs

These are graphs that represent a journey of some distance over some time or of some velocity over some time. The two **travel graphs** shown each represents a journey over one minute:

● A distance/time graph

● A velocity/time graph

Graphs from equations

Linear equations

All linear equations are of the form $y = mx + c$, where m and c are two constants. They are represented by a straight line graph of gradient m passing through the y axis at $y = c$ (the y axis intercept).

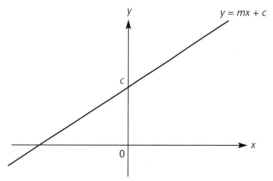

Graphs from linear equations

Quadratic equations

Graphs from quadratic equations of the form $y = ax^2 + bx + c$, where a, b and c are constants, are represented by a U-shaped curve.

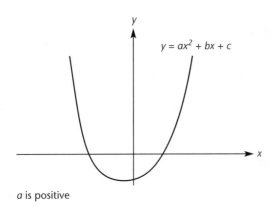

a is positive

We see that the pattern of the curve is different when a is positive rather than when a is negative. The solutions of the equation $ax^2 + bx + c = 0$ are the x axis intercepts.

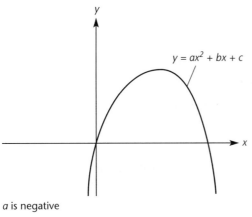

a is negative

Reciprocal equations

A reciprocal equation is of the form $y = A/x$ where A is a constant. A graph representing these equations will have the shape shown.

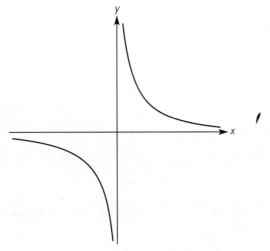

Graphs from reciprocal equations (hyperbola graphs)

‑‑‑ *Asymptotic, Reciprocal*

Graphs of inequalities

When drawing a graph of an ***inequality*** such as $y > 2x$ we need to indicate all the points on the grid where this inequality is true. There are a lot of points, but they will all fall on one side or the other of the straight line $y = 2x$.

If we were graphing the inequality $y \geqslant 2x$, the solution would include the points on the line $y = 2x$, whereas the solution of $y > 2x$ will not include the points on this line.

So to draw a region say $y < 3x$ we need to draw the line $y = 3x$, then to find which side of this line we want. One way of doing this is to choose some convenient point that is *not on the line*, say (0,2). (The *origin* (0,0) is always the simplest point to choose if you can, but of course in this case it is on the line itself, so you must choose another point). Substitute these values into the inequality and we get $2 < 0$; this is *not true*, so we shade-in the *other side* of the line rather than the side containing the point (0,2), as shown.

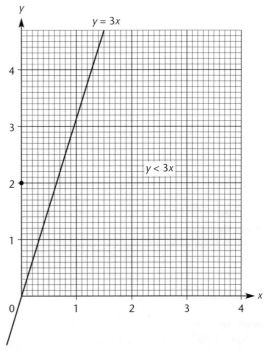

Graphs of inequalities

Exam Question

The diagrams show axes with the lines $y = x + 2$ and $x + y = 5$ both drawn and labelled.

(a) On copies of the diagram;
   (i) shade the region $y < x + 2$
   (ii) shade the region $x + y > 5$
(b) Draw a similar grid as above, and on it shade the region $x < 4$

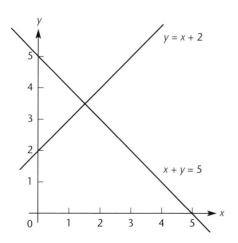

Solution

(a) (i)

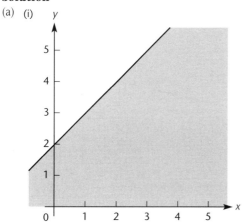

(ii)

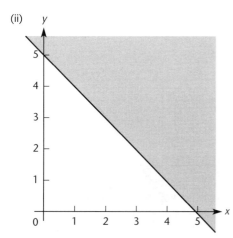

(b)

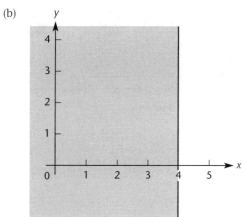

Sketch graphs

A sketch graph is a rough but reasonably accurate graph using as few points as possible to fix the main features of the graph. It is usually done by first recognizing what type of graph it will be, whether linear, quadratic, reciprocal or something else. Then, remembering the main features of that type of graph, the necessary points that will fix the shape onto a grid are calculated and the graph sketched.

Trigonometrical graphs

Each of the trigonometrical functions has a recognizable graph that you ought to be familiar with. (This is a Higher Level topic only).

Sine curve

The sine curve is the graph of $y = \sin x°$. Notice the main features are that

- it starts at the origin
- the highest value of y is 1
- the lowest value – 1.
- The curve has line symmetry about the line $x = 90°$ and $x = 270°$ although you would need to extend the graph both backwards and forwards to fully appreciate this.

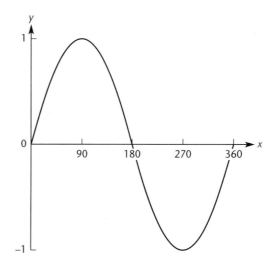

Sine curve

Cosine curve

The cosine curve representing $y = \cos x°$ is the same as the sine curve, only it has been translated 90° (to the left) along the x axis.

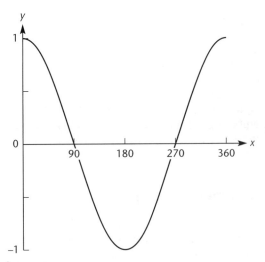

Cosine curve

Tangent curve

The tangent curves representing $y = \tan x°$ are quite different to the waves of the sine and the cosine. Notice the main feature of going through the origin (and $x = 180°$) and the strange effect at $x = 90°$ and $x = 270°$.

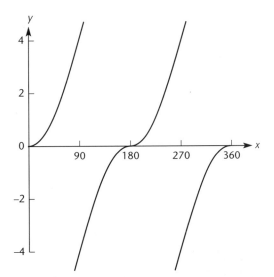

Tangent curve

It can be useful to know these trigonometrical shapes, especially when you may need to calculate a function of an angle larger than 90° or vice versa.

Exam Question
(a) Water is sucked at a constant rate into the pipette shown. On the axes provided, draw a sketch graph showing how the water level increases with time as the water is sucked to the level indicated on the drawing.

(NEAB; H)

(b) The velocity v m/s of the ball depicted rolling down a slope is give by $v = 3t$, where t seconds is the time after the ball is released.
   (i) Complete the table for values of v.
   (ii) Draw the graph of v against t for values of t from 0 to 5.
   (iii) Find the gradient of this graph.
   (iv) What does the gradient of this graph represent?

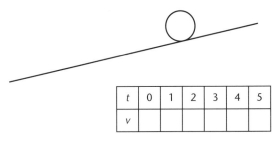

t	0	1	2	3	4	5
v						

(c) The graph and spring shown relate to a pupil's experiment. The total length (l) of a spring was measured when different masses were attached, and the results were plotted on the graph.

   Use the graph to find the equation linking the total length, l, with the mass, m, for this spring.

(NEAB; H)

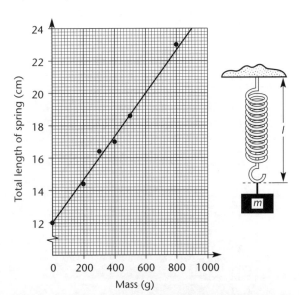

Solution
(a)

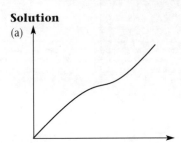

(b) (i) t 0, 1, 2, 3,   4, 5
        v 0, 3, 6, 9, 12, 15

(ii) v

(iii) Gradient = vertical distance ÷ horizontal distance = 15 ÷ 5 = 3

(iv) The acceleration.

(c) The equation is linear; hence the form of $l = am + c$ where a is the gradient of the line and c is the l axis intercept.
The gradient is found by $\frac{12}{900}$ = 0.013
The l intercept is 12; hence the equation will be $l = 0.013m + 12$.

Conversion graphs

-⊹- *Conversion graphs*

GROUPED DATA

-⊹- *Data*

HEXAGON

A hexagon is a *polygon* with 6 sides.

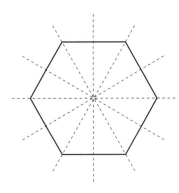

A regular hexagon will have 6 lines of **symmetry** and **rotational symmetry** of order 6.

The exterior angle is $360 \div 6 = 60°$
The interior angle is $180 - 60° = 120°$
The sum of its interior angles is $180 \times 4 = 720°$.

⊹ *Polygon*

CHECKPOINT

For a regular hexagon:

(a) How many lines of symmetry does it have?
(b) What is its order of rotational symmetry?
(c) What is the size of the exterior angle?
(d) What is the size of the interior angle?

HIGHEST COMMON FACTOR (HCF)

This is the highest of all the common **factors** of two or more whole numbers. For example, the common factors of 36 and 48 are 1, 2, 3, 4, 6 and 12. Since 12 is the highest, this is the highest common factor, or HCF for short.

HIRE PURCHASE

Usually called HP for short, hire purchase is sometimes called the 'never–never' or 'buy now, pay later'. It is a convenient way of spreading payment for goods over a period of some months or even years. It usually requires a **deposit** to be paid before the goods can be taken away and a promise

(contract) to pay so much each week or month, as necessary. For example:

> John bought his flute on HP. It originally cost £300, but the terms were £50 deposit and £15 a month for 24 months.

Note how the total paid was £50 + (15 × 24) which is £410. The HP price is *never* less than the original cost price.

HISTOGRAM

● A histogram is similar to a **bar chart**, but with the areas of the bars representing the frequency, and not the lengths of the bars.

● There should be no gaps between each bar in a histogram, as often happens with bar charts.

● Where the bars have unequal widths the vertical axis is a **frequency density** and not **frequency**, so that the frequency is found by multiplying the width of the bar by the number on the frequency density axis.

● The horizontal axis nearly always uses continuous data.

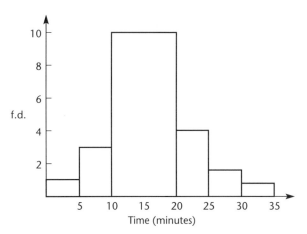

Histogram

> Remember: The area of the bars on the histogram represent the frequency – not the heights.

The histogram shown gives the waiting times that patients had at a doctor's surgery during one month. Notice how the waiting times between 10 and 20 minutes have been lumped together. Also notice that the smaller number of waits, between 0 and 5 minutes and 30 and 35 minutes, are such that we can still see them on the diagram without it looking ridiculous. From this histogram the groups are as in the table.

When drawing the horizontal scale we have to look carefully at the class intervals. The table below illustrates the clearest way to describe the above class intervals.

Waiting time (t)	f.d. × width	Frequency
$0 \leqslant t \leqslant 5$	1×5	$= 5$
$5 < t \leqslant 10$	3×5	$= 15$
$10 < t \leqslant 20$	10×10	$= 100$
$20 < t \leqslant 25$	4×5	$= 20$
$25 < t \leqslant 30$	1.6×5	$= 8$
$30 < t \leqslant 35$	0.8×5	$= 4$

The main concern is that there should be no doubt as to the group in which any piece of data will fall. So where the data is labelled 5, 10, 15 etc., it should be clear where values of 5, 10 and 15 actually are.

HYPERBOLA

A type of curve having two ***asymptotes***.

-‡- *Graphs*

HYPOTENUSE

This is the longest side of a right-angled triangle; it is to be found opposite the right angle. Its length is often found by the theorem of **Pythagoras**. This states that:

'the square of the hypotenuse is equal to the sum of the squares of the other two sides'; that is

$$h^2 = a^2 + b^2$$
$$h = \sqrt{a^2 + b^2}$$

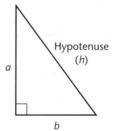

Hypotenuse

The hypotenuse is also used in trigonometry where:

$$\sin x = \frac{\text{side opposite}}{\text{hypotenuse}}$$

$$\cos x = \frac{\text{side adjacent}}{\text{hypotenuse}}$$

HYPOTHESIS

The term *hypothesis* refers to some theory. In statistics we often wish to *test* hypotheses or theories to see whether we can be confident that their predictions will hold true.

IMAGE

An image is the result of some mathematical **function** or a **transformation**. For example, in the function defined as f:$x \rightarrow 5x$ then the image of x is $5x$, and so the image of, say, 3 is 5×3 which is 15.

Another example is a **reflection** of a shape in the y axis. Its image is the shape drawn after the reflection. The term 'image set' is sometimes used for the **range**.

IMPERIAL

Imperial is the word used to describe the weights and measures that belong (or belonged) to the official British series of weights and measures. The common units that you ought to be familiar with are:

$$12 \text{ inches} = 1 \text{ foot}$$
$$3 \text{ feet} = 1 \text{ yard}$$
$$16 \text{ ounces} = 1 \text{ pound}$$
$$8 \text{ pints} = 1 \text{ gallon}$$

There are others, but these are the ones that you do need to have some familiarity with. You ought also to be aware of the following **metric** equivalences:

2 pounds weight	is approximately	1 kilogram
3 feet	is approximately	1 metre
5 miles	is approximately	8 kilometres
1 gallon	is approximately	4.5 litres

Exam Question
In 1997 the best time for running the mile was 221 seconds.
Take 5 miles to be equal to 8 kilometres.
Calculate what the time for the 1500 metres would have been, assuming that the average speed was the same.

Solution
$$1 \text{ mile} = 8 \div 5 = 1.6 \text{ km}$$
so 1600 metres = 221 seconds
$$1500 \text{ metres} = \frac{221}{1600} \times 1500 = 207 \text{ seconds (rounded)}$$

INCOME TAX

Income tax is the type of tax that everyone who receives enough money for working, or from investments, has to pay to the government. This amount can change every time the government decides to change it (usually in the Budget). To calculate the amount of income tax you should pay, you need to know the *rate of tax* (a percentage) and your *personal* allowance.

Rate of tax

The rate of tax is expressed as a percentage, for example 25%. This means that you would pay 25% of your *taxable income* to the government as tax. This rate is sometimes expressed as a rate in the £. For example, the rate of 25% could be expressed as 25p in the £.

Personal allowances

Personal allowances are the amounts of money you may earn *before* you start to pay tax. They are different for single men and married men (at the moment), and for women in different situations.

Taxable income

You only pay *income tax* on taxable income which is found by subtracting your personal allowances from your actual annual income. If your personal allowances are *greater than* your annual income, then you pay no income tax.

Here is an example of income tax calculation:

Mr Coefield, who earns £19,700 a year, has personal allowances totalling £4,300. What income tax does he pay in a year where the rate of tax is 25%?

The taxable income is 19,700 – 4,300 = 15,400
The income tax paid = 25% of £15,400 = £3,850

INDEX

An index is the figure that is found at the top right-hand corner of another number or algebraic expression to indicate a **power** (or **exponent**). The index tells us how many times that number is to be multiplied by itself. For example, $2^3 = 2 \times 2 \times 2$, the *three* being the index.

Standard index form

Standard index form is a convenient way of writing very large or very small numbers. It is always expressed in the terms of $A \times 10^N$ where A is a number between 1 and 10 and N is an **integer** (whole number). For example:

350	would be written as	3.5×10^2
413,200	would be written as	4.132×10^5
6,450.9	would be written as	6.4509×10^3

Notice how the index on the 10 tells you how many places *to the right* to move the decimal point.

If the number is less than 1 to start with, then the index on the 10 will be negative. Here the index will tell you how many places *to the left* to move the decimal point. For example:

0.045   would be written as 4.5×10^{-2}
0.0008   would be written as 8.0×10^{-4}

Standard form

Indices

Indices is the plural of index, and is the word used to describe the *set of numbers* written in this index notation, e.g. x^6.

Rules of indices

If the *base number* is the same in each case then:

- When you multiply indices you simply need to *add* their powers:

  i.e. $a^x \times a^y = a^{x+y}$
  e.g. $y^2 \times y^3 = y^{2+3} = y^5$

- When you divide indices you simply need to subtract their powers:

  i.e. $a^x \div a^y = a^{x-y}$
  e.g. $y^5 \div y^2 = y^{5-2} = y^3$

- You need to know that for any number x then $x^1 = x$ and $x^0 = 1$

- We use negative indices to show numbers of a fractional form. For example:

  $x^{-3} = 1/x^3$ and $3^{-2} = 1/3^2$

- Fractional indices can also be used to indicate *roots*. For example:

  $16^{\frac{1}{2}}$ will be $\sqrt{16}$ which is 4 and –4

  Also $x^{\frac{1}{3}}$ will indicate $\sqrt[3]{x}$ that is the cubed root of x. More generally the power $1/n$ will indicate the nth root.

- Note that a power such as 2/3 will indicate the square of the cubed root, or the cubed root of the square. For example:

  $27^{\frac{2}{3}} = \sqrt[3]{(27^2)} = \sqrt[3]{729} = 9$
  or $(\sqrt[3]{27})^2 = 3^2 = 9$

Exam Question
Find the value of x in each of the following equations:

(a) $2^x = 8$
(b) $2^x = \frac{1}{8}$
(c) $8^x = \frac{1}{2}$

(SEG; H)

Solution
(a) $x = 3$
(b) $x = -3$
(c) $x = -\frac{1}{3}$

Exam Question
Find the value of (i) 9^4
(ii) 5^{-2}

Solution
(i) $9 \times 9 \times 9 \times 9 = 6561$
(ii) $\dfrac{1}{5 \times 5} = 0.04$

CHECKPOINT

Put these numbers into standard index form:

(a) Six million
(b) 0.0075

INEQUALITIES

Inequalities are signs used to indicate how two expressions might be different in terms of their relative sizes:

$>$ means 'greater than', e.g. $5 > 2$
$<$ means 'less than', e.g. $3 < 6$
$\geqslant$ means 'greater than or equal to'
$\leqslant$ means 'less than or equal to'

INEQUATIONS

An inequation is an equation with an *inequality sign* in it; but the term **inequality** is often also used to describe an inequation. They are solved in much the same way as a normal equation is solved, except for when you wish to multiply or divide both sides by a *negative amount*. In this case you then have to *reverse* the inequality sign, for example $3 > 1$ would become $-3 < -1$. For example:

Find the range of values for which $2x - 7 > 3(5 - x)$

Using normal equation techniques we can calculate that
$2x - 7 > 15 - 3x$
to give $5x > 22$ so $x > 22/5$
hence the solution is $x > 4.4$

Remember: When solving inequations, you should treat them as normal equations with the same inequality sign as you started with.

Graphing inequations

Graphs of inequalities lead us into *solution sets*, which is when we need to find a solution to a *set* of inequations. In this case we would shade all unwanted regions, leaving ourselves with the possible solution set *unshaded*. For example:

Illustrate the set of points that satisfy the inequations: $x > 0$, $y > 0$, $x + y < 6$, $x + 3y > 6$

The $x > 0$ and the $y > 0$ indicate to us that we only need the region where both x and y are positive.

Hence shading out the other two regions leaves us with the possible points we are looking for.

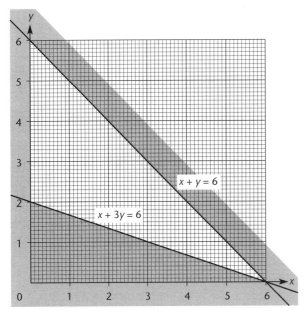

Graphing inequations

Always be aware of the inequality sign and remember to notice whether it is $>$ or $\geqslant$ etc. In the latter case you do need to include the points on the line in your solution set.

This is a difficult part of graph work and an area where a lot of mistakes are so easily made, especially in finding out the various regions and correctly shading them. Be very careful to check your inequations and to make certain that you are shading the correct region, as required by the situation.

Exam Question
1. Find the whole number values of n that satisfy the inequality
    $$8 \leqslant 5n + 7 < 19$$

2. Solve the inequality $x^2 < 9$

Solution
1. left-hand side; $8 \leqslant 5n + 7$
    $$8 - 7 \leqslant 5n$$
    $$\tfrac{1}{5} \leqslant n \quad \text{or} \quad 0.2 \leqslant n$$

    right-hand side; $5n + 7 < 19$
    $$5n < 19 - 7$$
    $$n < \tfrac{12}{5} \quad \text{or} \quad n < 2.4$$

    hence $0.2 \leqslant n < 2.4$

2. $x < 3$ and $x > -3$
    i.e. $-3 < x < 3$

┄┼┄ Graphs

INFINITE

This is a number that is far too big to be counted, or indeed, is uncountable; for example, the number of stars in the sky, or the number of grains of sand in the world, or the number of times you can take 0 away from 1 without getting a negative result. This last example indicates just why 1/0 is infinity and why, when you try it on your calculator, you get E for error, since the calculator cannot do it.

INTEGERS

An integer is a whole number like 1, 2, 3, 4 etc. It can be positive, zero or negative as with –1, –2, –3, etc.

INTERCEPT

An intercept is where a line crosses an axis; an intercept on the x axis is called an *x axis intercept*, and an intercept on the y axis a *y axis intercept*.

In the general equations of lines, the y axis intercept is given by the *constant* in the equation:

● For a linear equation of $y = mx + c$, then c is the y axis intercept

● For the *quadratic equation* of $y = ax^2 + bx + c$, again c is the y axis intercept.

These points can be most useful when sketching graphs.

INTEREST

Interest is what we call the amount of money that someone will give you for letting them borrow your money, or what you pay for borrowing money from someone else. So you can receive interest and you can *pay* interest.

Banks and building societies give you interest if you let them borrow some of your money. For example, if a bank pays 6.5% interest *per annum* (per year), then if you leave £30 in their bank for the one year, they will pay you $£30 \times \frac{6.5}{100} = £1.95$

Types of interest

There are two types of interest, simple and compound interest.

Simple interest

Simple interest (*SI*) is calculated on the basis of having a principal amount, say P, in the bank, for a number of years T, with a rate of interest R. There is then a formula to work out the amount of simple interest earned:

$$SI = PRT/100$$

In other words, you multiply the principal by the rate by the time and then divide by 100. For example:

Joseph had £14.50 in an account that paid simple interest at a rate of 8%. Calculate how much interest would be paid to Joseph if he kept the money in this account for 4 years.

The principal is £14.50, the rate is 8% and the time is 4 years.
Hence using the formula $SI = PRT/100 =$
$14.5 \times 8 \times 4/100$, which is £4.64

Compound interest

Compound interest (CI) is the type of interest most likely to be paid to you by banks and building societies. It is based on the idea of giving you the simple interest after 1 year and then adding this onto your principal amount (sometimes this interest is calculated and added every 6 months). The money then grows more quickly than it would with just simple interest. For example:

Helen paid £50 into a bank that paid her 5% interest every 6 months, adding this to the principal every 6 months. Calculate how much she has in the account after 2 years:

● After 6 months she earns interest of £50 × 5/100 which is £2.50; hence she will have £52.50

● After 12 months she earns interest of £52.50 × 5/100 which is £2.63; hence she will have £55.13

● After 18 months she earns interest of £55.13 × 5/100 which is £2.76; hence she will have £57.89

● After 2 years she earns interest of £57.89 × 5/100 which is £2.89; hence she will have £60.78

Note that there is a formula for working out compound interest:

$$CI = P \times (1 + \tfrac{R}{100})^N - P$$

where P = principal amount, R = rate of interest, N = number of times to be applied.
    The formula for the *final amount* earned in compound interest is:

$$\text{total interest} = P \times (1 + \tfrac{R}{100})^N$$

Notice how the formula is simpler if you want to find the whole amount. But it must be used with caution, because if the interest is actually paid into an account each year, or 6 months, etc., then rounding off will be taking place which will eventually give a slightly different answer to the formula. In an exam situation, either method of gaining the answer to compound interest will be acceptable; but you ought to be aware that there is a difference. Try this out on the example above if you wish to check for yourself.

Exam Question
In a savings account, compound interest is paid at 8.5% per year. Jim starts with £200 in his savings account. Calculate:

(a) how much interest will be paid in the first year,
(b) the total in his account after one year,
(c) how much interest will be paid in the second year,
(d) the total in his account after two years.

(NEAB; I)

Solution
(a) 8.5 × 200 ÷ 100 = £17
(b) 200 + 17 = £217
(c) 8.5 × 217 ÷ 100 = £18.45
(d) 217 + 18.45 = £235.45

INTERQUARTILE RANGE

This is the difference between the upper and lower *quartiles* on any cumulative frequency curve. It should be expressed simply as the number difference on the horizontal axis. For example, in the figure showing interquartile range:

the upper quartile is 20 and the lower quartile is 10.5, so the interquartile range is 20 – 10.5, which is 9.5.

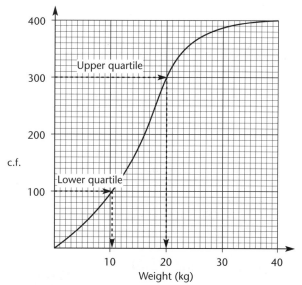

Interquartile range

The use of interquartile range is to define a range of marks and to see how a frequency distribution is spread out; it gives the position of the middle 50% of a population.

Semi-interquartile range

The semi-interquartile range is exactly what it says – half of the interquartile range. So, divide the interquartile range by two.

Exam Question
The cumulative frequency distributions are shown for the heights of two different types of mature (fully grown) corn, type A and type B.

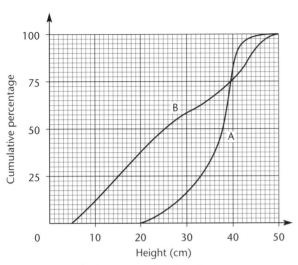

Two cumulative frequency distributions

(a) Complete the table below for the two types of corn.

	Median height (cm)	Upper quartile (cm)	Lower quartile (cm)	Interquartile range
Type A				
Type B				

(b) Comment briefly on the distributions of the height of the two types of corn.
(c) A mature corn plant is measured and found to have a height of 28 cm. State, with a reason, which of the two types of corn you think it is.

(NEAB; I)

Solution
(a)

	Median height (cm)	Upper quartile (cm)	Lower quartile (cm)	Interquartile range
Type A	37.5	39.5	33	6.5
Type B	25	39.5	15	24.5

(b) Type A will all grow to a similar height. Type B shows a wide spread of heights with little reliability in the growth.
(c) Type B is the more likely because only a small proportion of type A corn would be this small.

INVERSE TRANSFORMATION

An inverse of a **transformation** T is that transformation T' which, when combined with T, would leave any shape where it originally was.

● **Reflections** have what are called **self-inverses** since their inverses are themselves. For example, for a reflection in the line $y = x$, the *inverse* will be the same reflection in the same line.

Other transformations have simple-to-find inverses, for example:

● **Rotations** around a point through an angle x. Here the inverse will be another rotation around the same point, but through the angle $-x$.

● **Enlargements** of scale factor K through some point. Here the inverse will be another enlargement through the same point, but of scale factor $1/K$.

● **Translation** of a vector $\begin{pmatrix} a \\ b \end{pmatrix}$; here, the inverse will be another translation with a vector $\begin{pmatrix} -a \\ -b \end{pmatrix}$.

INVESTIGATIONS

These are mathematical enquiries where you need to search through selected data in order to find a pattern or a solution to some defined problem.

Investigations are best examined through **coursework** However, there will be an element of investigation within examination questions, particularly where you need to examine some number sequence.

In explaining any solution to your investigation, you must make all your reasons clear, stating *how* you found any relationships. For example:

Some numbers like 4 and 9 have exactly three factors and no more. Find the next three numbers like these to have exactly three factors.

After a short search, you should find that 25 is the next number to have exactly three factors. Note that the solutions involve square numbers but only the squares of **prime numbers**; so the next two such numbers are 7×7 and 11×11. Hence the next three numbers are 25, 49 and 121, but you should have *stated the reasons* why these are the next three numbers.

Exam Question
The questions below refer to the numbers in the grid.

```
 0    3    6    9   12   ...
 4    7   10   13   16   ...
 8   11   14   17   20   ...
12   15   18   21   24   ...
16   19   22   25   28   ...
 .    .    .    .    .
 .    .    .    .    .
 .    .    .    .    .
```

The diagonal difference for any 2×2 square on the grid is defined as $qs - pr$, where p, q, r and s are numbers in the square as shown below.

p	q
s	r

Squares are identified by the number in the top left-hand corner. This square is called a 'p' square.

(a) Find the diagonal difference for the '14' square.
(b) Investigate the diagonal difference for *two* other squares on the grid. Write down your results and any observations that you can make.

(NEAB; H)

Solution

(a) The 14 square is:

14	17
18	21

The diagonal difference is $(18 \times 17) - (14 \times 21) = 12$

(b) The other two you did will also give you a diagonal difference of 12. It looks as though you will always get a diagonal difference of 12.

IRRATIONAL

An irrational number is one that *cannot* be expressed as a ***vulgar fraction***, i.e. as a/b, where both a and b are integers (whole numbers). It is also true to say that an irrational number *cannot* be expressed as a ***terminating*** or ***recurring*** decimal.

The most commonly encountered examples of irrational numbers are π and $\sqrt{2}$. (This is a Higher Level only topic.)

> *Remember: All multiples of π are irrational also.*

CHECKPOINT

Which of the following numbers are irrational?

$\sqrt{3}$, 0.77, $(\pi - 3)$, $\frac{3}{4}$, 5π

ISOSCELES

An isosceles triangle has two of its sides the same length and two angles the same. The line that bisects the angle included between the two sides of the same length is a ***line of symmetry*** and is ***perpendicular*** to the line facing the angle. This is useful to know when asked to find angle sizes or lengths, since you can then use ***trigonometry***.

An isosceles triangle

Example

Find the size of angle x in the figure.

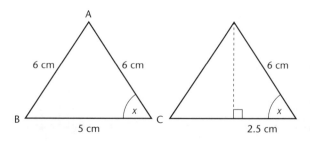

Solution

First, drop a perpendicular down from A to BC. This will divide the triangle in half, to give us the right-angled triangle as shown. Now use trigonometry to calculate the size of angle x as 65.4°.

ITERATION

An iteration is when some generating term, U_n, is used to keep on generating terms until a certain situation is satisfied. For example, a solution to the equation $x^2 - 2x - 3 = 0$ can be found by re-writing the equation in the form: $x^2 = 3 + 2x$, then in the form:

$$x = \frac{3}{x} + 2$$

Suppose we guess an approximate starting solution X_1 to this equation as being $X_1 = 2$. We now find the value this starting approximation makes the left-hand side of the equation. We will find that:

$$X_2 = \frac{3}{X_1} + 2 = 3/2 + 2 = 3.5$$

We then use this value of $X_2 = 3.5$ as a better approximate solution in the equation. We now get $X_3 = 3/3.5 + 2 = 2.857...$

By continuing the process we find that:

$$X_4 = 3.05$$
$$X_5 = 2.98$$
$$X_6 = 3.01$$
$$X_7 = 3.00$$
$$X_8 = 3.00$$

The process was continued *until* the value to 2 decimal places was the same two times in succession. The actual calculator value was used each time in the iteration. Hence the solution here is $x = 3$, which can be shown to be correct by substituting it into the original equation.

This type of question in an examination will almost certainly start by leading you to the first starting solution. The most common error for candidates to make is to *round off* in the middle of the iteration, instead of keeping the correct values in the calculator. By all means show rounded off values in your method of solution, but keep as accurate a value as possible in your calculator.

Exam Question

(a) The iterative formula $U_{n+1} = \frac{1}{10}(12 - U_n^2)$ is used to generate a sequence of numbers, given the value of U_1. Given that $U_1 = 1$, find U_2, U_3, U_4 and U_5, giving your answers to U_4 and U_5 correct to four places of decimals.

(b) Using the formula for solving quadratic equations, solve the equation $x^2 + 10x - 12 = 0$ correct to two places of decimals.

   Comment on the relationship between your solution to this equation and your answers to part (a).

(NEAB; H)

Solution

(a) $U_2 = 0.1(12 - 1^2) = 1.1$
   $U_3 = 0.1(12 - 1.1^2) = 1.079$
   $U_4 = 0.1(12 - 1.079^2) = 1.0836$
   $U_5 = 0.1(12 - U_4^2) = 1.0826$

(b) Use $x = \dfrac{-b \pm \sqrt{(b^2 - 4ac)}}{2a}$

   $= \dfrac{-10 \pm \sqrt{(100 + 48)}}{2} = -11.08$ and 1.08

The positive solution of 1.08 is the same as the solution to the iteration.

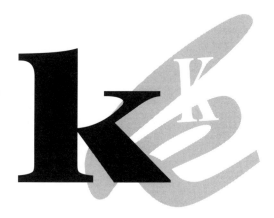

KITE

A kite, recognizable as the shape of a kite, has four sides, with the top two sides the same length and the bottom two sides the same length.

A kite will have one **line of symmetry** bisecting the angles included between the sides of the same length.

The area of a kite can be calculated by multiplying both diagonal lengths together and halving the result.

$$\text{area} = \tfrac{1}{2} \times 5 \times 8 = 20 \text{ cm}^2$$

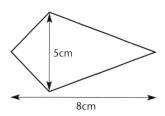

LENGTH

Length is a distance from one particular point to another. The length of a line is the distance from one *end* to the other. Examination questions often ask you to find a length; you usually need to use either **trigonometry** or the theorem of **Pythagoras**.

LINEAR

'Linear' has to do with being straight, so a line that is linear is straight The general equation of a linear line is $y = mx + c$ where m is the gradient of the straight line and c is the y axis intercept This **equation** is called a *linear equation*.

✦ *Equation, Graph, Sequence*

LINE OF BEST FIT

A line of best fit is the line that is drawn on a **scatter diagram** that best appears to represent the trend of the situation being graphed. This line is normally drawn as a *straight line*, but not necessarily so; it could be *curved* if that is what the trend is. However, the line of best fit is always the simplest line that could be drawn.

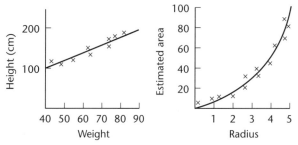

Line of best fit

Look at the two scatter diagrams shown. The line of best fit has been drawn in both cases. Note how one is a straight line and the other a curve.

Strictly speaking, the line of best fit is that line which minimizes the sum of squared deviations from the line. In later statistics courses you can use a formula to find the line of best fit.

LINE OF SYMMETRY

If you can fold a shape over so that one half fits exactly on top of the other half, then the line over which you have folded is called a line of symmetry. The examples shown illustrate the lines of symmetry in various shapes as dotted lines.

- The square has four lines of symmetry,
- the rectangle two,
- the isosceles triangle just one, as has the pentagon next to it,
- the circle has thousands and thousands of lines of symmetry: there are too many for us to count (we call this an infinite number).

Often, of course, you cannot fold over a shape that you are looking at, so you either have to imagine it being folded or trace it on tracing paper and then fold it. In most examinations you would be allowed to trace the shape and fold it over to find lines of symmetry.

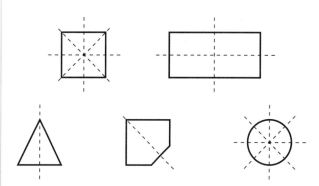

Lines of symmetry

> Remember: An **n**-sided regular polygon will have **n** lines of symmetry.

CHECKPOINT

How many lines of symmetry does a regular 18-sided polygon have?

LOCUS

A locus is the collection of all possible points relating to some rule. For example, the locus of all points 2 cm away from a dot is a *circle* of radius 2 cm with that dot as its centre.

Generally, to find a locus we can fix some points on a drawing and go on fixing more and more points until we see a pattern emerging which we can then say is the *locus* of the points. For example:

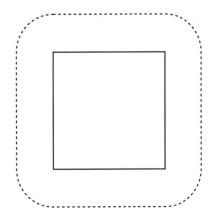

Locus

Find the locus of the points 1 cm away from, and outside, the square, of side 3 cm, shown above. The locus is the dotted line and was found by fixing in all those points 1 cm away from the edges of the square. Around each *vertex* there is a quarter-circle, meeting lines which are parallel to, and equal in length with, each side.

The most common mistake to be made on locus questions is for students to think they have a pattern before trying it out fully. As a result, only *part* of a pattern is often found, which of course is a wrong locus and so few marks would be gained.

Exam Question

A rectangular yard adjacent to a factory is patrolled by a guard dog, D, tethered by a chain 20 m long attached at the mid-point, M, of the factory wall, SR.

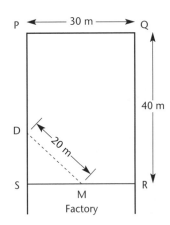

(a) Assuming the dog keeps the chain taut, sketch on the diagram the locus of the dog's path as it moves from one side of the yard to the other.
(b) Calculate the distance PM.
(c) An intruder climbs into the yard at P. Mark on the diagram the point N at which the dog is closest to the intruder. Calculate the distance PN.

(NEAB; I)

Solution

(a)

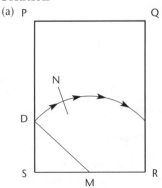

(b) By Pythagoras: $PM^2 = 40^2 + 15^2 = 1825$
so
$PM = \sqrt{1825} = 42.7$ m.
(c) See N on the diagram, then
PN will be:
$42.7 - 20 = 22.7$ m

Exam Question

This diagram shows a car park with two ticket machines A and B. People always go to the ticket machine nearest to them. Shade the region of the park from which people go to ticket machine B.

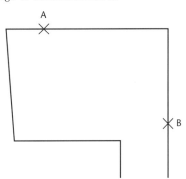

Solution

You need to construct the perpendicular bisector of the line AB first, then shade that part nearer to B

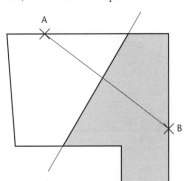

✛ *Bisect, Constructions*

LOWEST COMMON MULTIPLE

The lowest common multiple (LCM) of a set of *integers* is the smallest integer that can be divided exactly by each of the integers in the set. For example, the lowest common multiple of 4, 6 and 8 is 24, since 24 is the smallest integer that each of the integers 4, 6 and 8 will divide into exactly.

Remember: To find the middle mark of a group, you just add up the two end numbers and divide by 2.

MEAN

The mean usually refers to the *arithmetic mean*, which is the most common type of **average**. In fact it is usually what people are referring to when they say the average.

The mean of a set of numeric data is the sum of all the data divided by the total frequency of the data. In other words, it is the sum of all the numbers divided by how many numbers there are. For example, to find the mean of 4, 6, 3, 2, 7, 12, 8, 5, 13 and 9, you add up all the numbers to give you 69. Then divide by the number of numbers, which is 10, to give a mean of 6.9

Estimated mean

An estimated mean is found from a *grouped* frequency distribution where we do not know all the individual items of data. We only know how many items of data are between certain limits. For example, consider the grouped frequency in the table below.

Marks	Frequency
0–10	3
11–20	7
21–30	19
31–40	8

This shows the number of candidates obtaining various ranges of marks in an examination. To *estimate* the mean, we assume that each candidate scored the middle mark in each range. We then estimate the total marks for that group by multiplying the middle mark by the frequency.

We can now add up all these estimates to find how many the total data adds up to. Then divide this by the total frequency to obtain our estimated mean.

The table below shows how we have done this in this example. Here we estimate the mean as 892 ÷ 37 = 24 (rounded).

Marks	Midway m	Frequency f	m × f
0–10	5	3	15
11–20	15.5	7	108.5
21–30	25.5	19	484.5
31–40	35.5	8	284
Totals		37	892

Exam Question

A survey was carried out at a clinic during part of one day to see how long it took nurses to weigh and assess babies. The recorded times to the nearest minute, were as follows:

6	24	11	12	7
18	13	16	17	13
17	19	23	8	19
18	9	17	17	13
16	16	12	12	21

(a) (i) Calculate the mean time taken by the nurses to weigh and assess a baby on this day at the clinic.
   (ii) On average, how many babies could be assessed and weighed by one nurse during a three-hour session?

(b) The clinic usually has around 80 babies to weigh and assess each day in a morning session between 9 a.m. and 12 noon. Using your answers to part (a), calculate the number of nurses needed for each morning session.

(NEAB; I)

Solution

(a) (i) Add up all the times to calculate the mean as 374 ÷ 25 = 14.96 = 15 minutes.
   (ii) 3 × 60 = 180 minutes, then 180 ÷ 15 = 12 babies per session.

(b) 80 ÷ 12 = 6.67 hence 7 nurses would be needed.

Exam Question

The table shows the time it took cross country runners to finish a race.

Time (nearest minute)	Number of runners
40 < time ≤ 50	15
50 < time ≤ 70	20
70 < time ≤ 90	25
90 < time ≤ 100	30

Calculate an estimate for the mean time of the runners to finish the race.

Solution

You need to construct another column in the table of 'midway value × frequency'.
Then use this to estimate the total times divided by the total frequency.

Time (nearest minute)	Number of runners (frequency)	midway × frequency
40 < time ≤ 50	15	45 × 15 = 675
50 < time ≤ 70	20	60 × 20 = 1200
70 < time ≤ 90	25	80 × 25 = 2000
90 < time ≤ 100	30	95 × 30 = 2850
Totals	90	6725

estimated mean = 6725 ÷ 90 = 74.7 minutes.

MEDIAN

The median is another type of average. It is the middle item of data, once that data has been sorted into an order of size. If there are two items of data in the middle, as there will be with an even number of items, then we add them together and divide by 2 to calculate the median. In general, if there are N numbers in a frequency distribution, then the middle item is the $\frac{(N + 1)}{2}$ th.

For example, here are 15 test results. What is the median score?

81, 63, 59, 71, 36, 99, 56, 31, 5, 65, 46, 83, 71, 53, 15

Put the marks into order (5, 15, 31, 36, 46, 53, 56, 59, 63, 65, 71, 71, 81, 83, 99). Now find the middle one, which is 59. So the median score is 59.

Estimated median

The estimated median for a frequency distribution can be found by using a cumulative frequency graph. You can then read off what the middle item of data would be.

-✛- ***Average, Cumulative frequency***

MENSURATION

Mensuration is the study of the rules of measuring. Within any GCSE course you will be examined on how well you can measure lengths, areas and volumes.

This will include knowing simple area and volume formulae; you will also need to know *where to find* other formula on the *formula sheet* that you will be presented with in the examination. Of course the more formulae you can learn off by heart, instead of having to use the formula sheet, the easier and quicker you will be able to answer the examination questions.

You also need to be able to *recognize* those situations where you can use a right-angled triangle to find lengths by either **trigonometry** or by the theorem of **Pythagoras**. If an *angle* is given, use trigonometry; whereas if *two sides* are given, then use Pythagoras.

Exam Question

(a) A circle is contained within a square as shown. The radius of the circle is 5 cm. Estimate the area of the shaded part of the diagram. (Take the value of π to be 3)

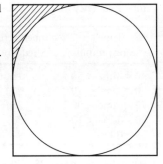

(SEG; I)

(b) Two closed cylindrical cans, A and B are shown. The radius of A is 4 cm and its height is 12 cm. The radius of B is 8 cm and its height is 6 cm.

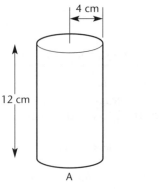
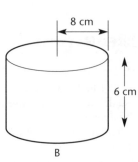

(i) Find, in the form 1: n, the ratios:

Volume of A : volume of B
Total surface area of A : total surface area of B

(ii) Two cylinders have the same volume. The first has radius r and height h. Given that the radius of the second is $2r$, find its height in terms of h.

(MEG; H)

Solutions

(a) The area of the rectangle = $10 \times 10 = 100$ cm^2
the area of the circle = $3 \times 25 = 75$ cm^2
shaded area = $(100 - 75) \div 4 = 6.25$ cm^2

(b) (i) Volume of A = $12\pi16 = 192\pi$
volume of B = $6\pi64 = 384\pi$
hence ratio of A:B = 192:384 = 1:2
Surface area of A = $\pi \times 8 \times 12 + 2 \times \pi \times 16 = 128\pi$
surface area of B = $\pi \times 16 \times 6 + 2 \times \pi \times 64 = 224\pi$
hence ratio of A:B = 128:224 = 1:1.75

(ii) Volume of first = πr^2h
volume of second = $\pi(2r)^2H$.
Then $\pi4r^2H = \pi r^2h$
hence $H = \frac{\pi r^2 h}{4\pi r^2} = \frac{h}{4}$

METRIC

The metric units are the ones that have been used throughout the rest of Europe for quite a while. Britain is trying to encourage its population to use metric units rather than **imperial** units. You ought to know and be familiar with the following metric unit facts:

● 1 kilogram = 1000 grams   or 1 kg = 1000 g

● 1 kilometre = 1000 metres   or 1 km = 1000 m

● 1 kilowatt = 1000 watts   or 1 kW = 1000 w

> *Remember: It is worth remembering that kilo means 1000.*

Other metric facts you ought to be aware of:

- 1000 kilograms = 1 tonne   or 1000 kg = 1 t
- 10 millimetres = 1 centimetre or 10 mm = 1 cm
- 100 centimetres = 1 metre   or 100 cm = 1 m
- 1000 millilitres = 1 litre   or 1000 ml = 1 l

It is very useful to be aware of the *rough equivalents* of metric and imperial units:

- 2 pounds weight is   approximately equal to 1 kilogram
- 3 feet   are   approximately equal to 1 metre
- 5 miles   are   approximately equal to 8 kilometres
- 1 gallon   is   approximately equal to 4.5 litres

A knowledge of these conversion factors is not needed, but a familiarity with them is useful as they could crop up in an examination question. Such familiarity will also be useful in the real world of work.

Imperial

Exam Question

Billie's mother sends him to the shops to buy 4 pounds of potatoes and 3 pints of milk. He buys a 3 kilogram bag of potatoes and a litre carton of milk. Does he buy enough potatoes and milk?

Solution

Potatoes; 3 kg = 3 × 2.2 pounds = 6.6 pounds, yes this is enough potatoes.

Milk 1 gallon = 8 pints = 4.5 litres,

so 3 pints = $3 \times \frac{4.5}{8}$ = 1.68 litres. No, he has not

enough milk.

CHECKPOINT

How many:

(a) Square millimetres are there in a square centimetre?
(b) Square centimetres are there in a square metre?
(c) Cubic centimetres in a cubic metre?

MIXED NUMBERS

A mixed number is one which is written with two distinct parts; one part includes a whole number, while the other part is the **vulgar fraction**. For example $5\frac{2}{3}$ is a mixed number.

To change a 'top heavy' fraction into a mixed number, you need to divide the bottom number

(denominator) into the top number (numerator) and find any remainder, e.g.:

$$\frac{29}{8} \rightarrow 29 \div 8 = 3 \text{ remainder } 5 \rightarrow 3\frac{5}{8}$$

To change a mixed number to a **decimal** number, start with the vulgar fraction. Then, using your calculator, divide the numerator (top number) by the denominator (bottom number); add to your result the whole number part of the mixed number.

For example, to change $4\frac{3}{8}$ to a decimal we would use the calculator to divide 3 by 8 to get 0.375, then add 4 to this, giving us 4.375. This is the decimal equivalent of $4\frac{3}{8}$.

MODE

The mode is a type of **average**; it is what most people have. The mode is the value occurring most times in a particular frequency distribution. The number 1 hit single each week is the record that has sold more copies than any other record that week; it is therefore the mode record or, as it is sometimes called, the *modal* record.

- In a **bar chart**, the mode is always the data represented by the longest bar.
- In a **pie chart**, the mode is the data represented by the largest sector (the largest angle).

> Remember: In grouped frequency the modal group is the one containing the highest frequency.

MULTIPLES

The multiples of an **integer**, say *N*, are the integers that will divide exactly by *N*. In other words, they will be the results from the *N*-times table. For example, the multiples of 5 are 5, 10, 15, 20, 25, etc.

Common multiples

The common multiples of two or more integers are those integers that can be divided exactly by these integers. For example, the common multiples of 5 and 3 are 15, 30, 45, etc., as these numbers can be divided exactly by *both* 3 and 5.

Lowest common multiple

The **lowest common multiple** (LCM) is the smallest of the common multiples. In the example above the LCM is 15.

MULTIPLYING/MULTIPLICATION

Directed numbers

NEGATIVE ENLARGEMENTS

⟡ *Enlargements*

NEGATIVE NUMBERS

Negative numbers are those found on a thermometer below freezing point. They have a *negative* (minus) *sign* to go with them, so that we know they are negative numbers.

Any number smaller than 0 is a negative number.

⟡ *Directed numbers*

> Remember: If you multiply two negative numbers you get a positive answer. If you add two negative numbers you get a negative answer.

NEGATIVE SCALE FACTOR

⟡ *Enlargements*

NETS

A net is a flat shape that can be folded up to create a solid shape. You need to be able to *recognize* what shape a net will fold into. You must also be able to draw a net for any of the usual, regular, three-dimensional shapes; for example **cubes**, **cuboids**, **polyhedra**, **pyramids**, **cylinders** and **cones**.

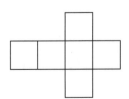
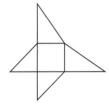

Nets

> Remember: Notice we do **not** put the flaps onto the edges of the shape. If we wanted to actually make a 3D shape from our net then we would need to put the flaps onto the net.

The question may give you a *net* and ask you to identify or draw the *shape* it will make, or it may ask you to draw a sketch of a *net* for some particular *shape*.

The most common mistake is for candidates to fail to visualize the three-dimensional shape that a net makes, and to answer the question with a two-dimensional shape. There are of course, for each solid shape, quite a few different ways to draw the net; all correct but different.

Exam Question
The closed packet sketched measures 30 cm by 18 cm by 7 cm. Sketch a net for this packet, marking in the dimensions.

(NISEAC; I)

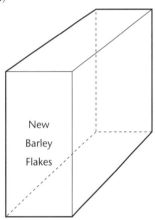

Solution
The answer sketched is not unique; there are a number of different possibilities.

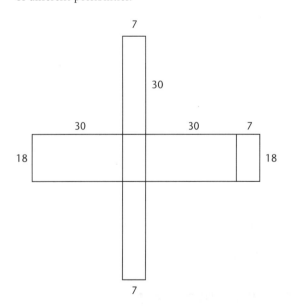

Exam Question
The diagram shows a square-based pyramid.
Each edge is 4 cm long.
Draw an accurate net of the tetrahedron.

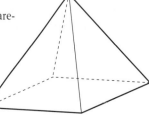

Solution

This is not a unique solution, but perhaps the simplest to draw.

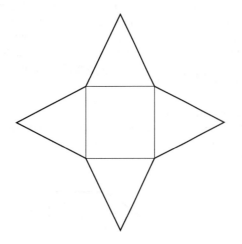

CHECKPOINT

A tetrahedron is a shape with every face an equilateral triangle.

Draw the net of a tetrahedron.

NONAGON

A nonagon is a nine-sided polygon.
The sum of its interior angles is $180 \times 7 = 1260°$
A regular nonagon will have 9 lines of symmetry and rotational symmetry of order 9

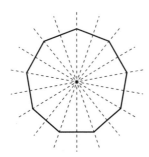

The exterior angle is $360 \div 9 = 40°$
The interior angle is $180 - 40 = 140°$

✦ *Polygon*

NUMBER PATTERNS

Both in coursework and in your final end of course examination, you will be expected to investigate, work out and recognize a variety of number patterns. Some of these will be based on the following:

● **Prime numbers**
2, 3, 5, 7, 11, 13, 17, 19, 23, 29...

● **Multiples**
3, 6, 9, 12, 15, 18, 21, 24, 27, 30...

● **Square numbers**
1, 4, 9, 16, 25, 36, 49, 64, 81, 100...

Searching for patterns

The most common way is to look at the *differences* between successive terms. This will in fact help you to find most of the patterns and then to continue them. For example, find the next three numbers in the following number pattern:

3, 7, 11, 15, 19...

Looking at the *differences* we see that the difference is four each time; so the pattern can be continued by simply adding on 4 each time, to give 23, 27 and 31.

Here is another example. Find the next three numbers in the number pattern:

8, 9, 11, 14, 18, 23...

Looking at the *differences* we see that they get bigger each time by one, so the next three numbers will be 29, 36 and 44.

Exam Question

Look at the following pattern. There is a figure missing in the last line.

$$1 \times 1 = 1$$
$$11 \times 11 = 121$$
$$111 \times 111 = 12321$$
$$1111 \times 1111 = 1234321$$
$$11111 \times 11111 = 1234*4321$$

(a) What figure should * be?
(b) Complete the answer for this line of the pattern.

$$111111 \times 111111 =$$

(c) Write down the next complete line of the pattern.

Solution

(a) 5
(b) 12345654321
(c) $1111111 \times 1111111 = 1234567654321$

Exam Question

(a) Write down the next two numbers in the number pattern

3, 8, 13, 18, 23 ...

(b) Write down in words what you think the rule is for finding the next number in the pattern from the one before it.
(c) Write down what you think the rule is for finding the nth number in the pattern.

Solution

(a) the next two numbers are 28 and 33
(b) add 5 onto the previous term.
(c) the difference is 5, the difference between the difference and the first term is 2, so the nth term is $5n - 2$.

✦ *Generalize, Sequence*

NUMBERS

Numbers may take a variety of forms.

Irrational numbers

An **irrational number** is one that cannot be expressed as a vulgar fraction, i.e. as $\frac{a}{b}$, where both a and b are integers (whole numbers). It is also true to say that any irrational number cannot be expressed as either a **terminating decimal** or a **recurring decimal**.

The most commonly quoted examples of irrational numbers are π and $\sqrt{2}$.

Prime numbers

A **prime number** is an integer that has exactly two **factors**; these two factors will of course always be the number itself and 1.

The first few prime numbers are 2, 3, 5, 7, 11, 13, 17, 19, 23, 29 and 31. You ought to be familiar with the numbers which are prime numbers and to note that 1 is not a prime number as it does not have two factors, only one.

Rational numbers

A **rational number** is a number that *can* be expressed as a vulgar fraction, i.e. as $\frac{a}{b}$, where a and b are both integers. It is true to say that every rational number is either a **terminating decimal** or a **recurring decimal**.

Real numbers

A **real number** is any number from the combination of the rational and irrational numbers. Every number that you come across in a GCSE course or examination will be a real number.

Square numbers

A **square number** is a number that can be formed by multiplying a whole number by itself. For example, 16 is a square number because 4 multiplied by itself is 16.

The first ten square numbers 1, 4, 9, 16, 25, 36, 49, 64, 81, 100 ought to be known.

There will be few questions that test specific knowledge of the above numbers; they are more likely to be examined *within* a question.

-+- *Directed number*

OCTAGON

An octagon is an eight-sided **polygon**. The sum of its interior angles is $180 \times 6 = 1{,}080°$. A regular octagon will have eight **lines of symmetry**, and **rotational symmetry** of order eight.

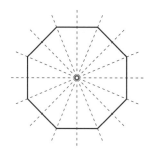

The exterior angle is $360 \div 8 = 45°$
The interior angle is $180 - 45 = 135°$

⤚ *Polygon*

OGIVE

The ogive is the special shape that you get on a cumulative frequency curve. On the cumulative curve shown the curved line is the *ogive*. From it you could evaluate the **quartiles** and the **median** of this distribution.

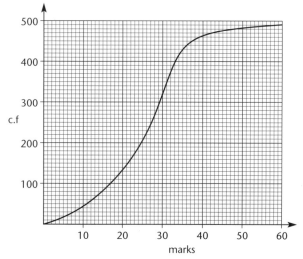

Ogive

Exam Question

Laura and Joy played 40 games of golf together.
The table below shows Laura's scores

Scores x	$70 < t \leq 80$	$80 < t \leq 90$	$90 < t \leq 100$	$100 < t \leq 110$	$110 < t \leq 120$
Frequency	1	4	15	17	3

(a) Draw a cumulative frequency diagram to show Laura's marks.
(b) Making your method clear, use your graph to find
  (i) Laura's median score.
  (ii) The interquartile range of her scores.
(c) Joy's median score was 103
  The interquartile range of her score was 6
  (i) Who was the more consistent player?
    Give a reason for your choice.
  (ii) The winner of a game of golf is the one with the lowest score.
    Who won most of these 40 games?
    Give a reason for your choice.

Solution
(a) The cumulative frequency is 1, 5, 20, 37, 40
  The cumulative frequency diagram is then;

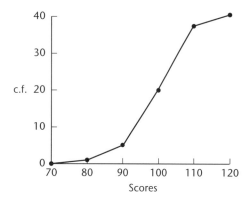

(b) (i) median = 100 (reading from 20 on the c.f.)
  (ii) lower quartile read from 10 on c.f. at 93.5
    upper quartile read from 30 on c.f. at 106
    the interquartile range is $106 - 93.5 = 12.5$
(c) (i) Joy is more consistent because she has a smaller interquartile range.
  (ii) Laura is likely to have won most games because she has a lower median.

OPPOSITE

Opposite is the word given to that side of a right-angled triangle opposite the angle that is being calculated by **trigonometry** (or has been given, and where you are using trigonometry to calculate a side).

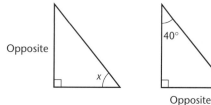

'OR' RULE

The 'OR' rule comes from the topic of **probability**. To find the probability of event A *or* event B, the probability of each event is *added* together.

67

However, these two events must be *mutually exclusive*, that is to say they cannot possibly happen at the same time. For example, in a bag that contains 5 toffees, 4 jellies and 3 mints, what is the probability of selecting one at random and it being a jelly or a mint?

The probabilities are:

Selecting a jelly $\frac{4}{12}$
Selecting a mint $\frac{3}{12}$
add these two together to get $\frac{7}{12}$

So probability of selecting a jelly *or* a mint = $\frac{7}{12}$.

> Remember: In most cases in the examination, the **OR** routine will be assessed at the same time as the **AND** routine through a combined event.

CHECKPOINT

What is the probability of cutting a pack of cards and getting either an ace or a king?

✦ **Combined events**

PARALLEL

Two lines are parallel if the **perpendicular** difference between them is always the same. Parallel lines are usually thought of as straight lines, but do not have to be. Two *circles* of different radii but the same centre are parallel with each other, but they are not straight lines. Some examples of parallel lines are shown.

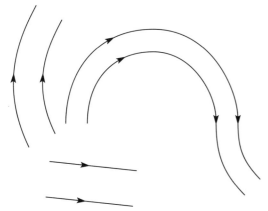

Parallel lines

PARALLELOGRAM

A parallelogram has four sides and the opposite sides are of equal length. The opposite sides are parallel. In a parallelogram any two angles next to each other will always add up to 180°, e.g.:

$$a + b = b + c = c + d = d + a = 180°$$

Also, the angles *opposite each other* will be equal. For example, $a = c$, $b = d$.

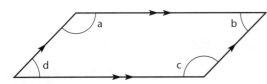

Parallelogram

The *area* of a parallelogram is found by multiplying the base length by the perpendicular height.

The most common error in finding the area of a parallelogram is multiplying the base length by the slant height.

In order to find the area of the parallelogram shown you need to use **trigonometry** to calculate the perpendicular height of the parallelogram. Then multiply this perpendicular height by the base length.

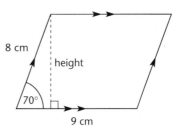

Exam Question

Draw, on a 1 cm dotted grid a parallelogram of area 12 cm².

(NEAB; I)

Solution

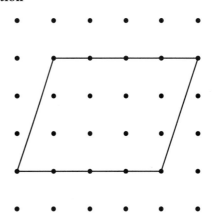

PASCAL'S TRIANGLE

Pascal's triangle is a particular triangular array of numbers, as follows:

								Row sum		
1st row					1				$= 2^0$	$= 1$
2nd row				1		1			$= 2^1$	$= 2$
3rd row			1		2		1		$= 2^2$	$= 4$
4th row		1		3		3		1	$= 2^3$	$= 8$
5th row	1		4		6		4	1	$= 2^4$	$= 16$

Try to write down (a) the 6th row and row sum; (b) the 11th row sum.

You should be able to see how the pattern builds itself down to give the 6th row as $1 + 5 + 10 + 10 + 5 + 1$, with a row sum of $32 = 2^5$.

Look at the number of the row and the row sum, and you should see that the row sum of the nth row is 2^{n-1}. Hence the row sum of the 11th row will be 2^{11-1} which is 2^{10}. Now, 2^{10} is $2^5 \times 2^5$, which is 32×32, which is 1,024, i.e. the row sum will be $1,024 = 2^{10}$.

Also, looking diagonally down the columns you will see the triangular numbers as well as some polyhedral numbers.

PENTAGON

A pentagon is a five-sided polygon. The sum of its interior angles is $180 \times 3 = 540°$. A regular pentagon has 5 **lines of symmetry** and **rotational symmetry** of order 5.

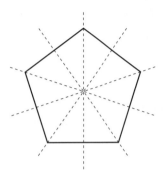

The exterior angle is $360 \div 5 = 72°$
The interior angle is $180 - 72 = 108°$

PERCENTAGES

One percent, written as 1%, means one out of one hundred, or $\frac{1}{100}$ or 0.01

Similarly 3% means 3 out of 100, or $\frac{3}{100}$, or 0.03, while 27% means 27 out of 100, or $\frac{27}{100}$, or 0.27

For example, to find 35% of £8 we calculate $8 \times \frac{35}{100} = £2.80$

Percentage calculations

Fractions to percentages

To change any *fraction* into a percentage, simply multiply that fraction by 100. For example, to change $\frac{15}{35}$ into a percentage, calculate on your calculator $\frac{15}{35} \times 100$ to give 42.9% (rounded off).

Percentage decrease

If we wish to *decrease* an amount by, say, 16%, then we really need to calculate $(100 - 16)\%$ or 84% of the amount.

For example, to decrease £9 by 14%, first recognize that this decrease is really $100 - 14$ which is 86%; then calculate on your calculator $9 \times \frac{86}{100}$ which is £7.74

Of course there is another way to do this which simply requires you to calculate 14% of £9 and then to *subtract* this from £9, but this is a much longer method.

Percentage increase

If we wish to *increase* an amount by say 8%, then we really need to calculate 108% of the amount.

For example, to increase £15 by 8% simply calculate on the calculator $15 \times \frac{108}{100}$ which gives £16.20

The longer method would simply require you to calculate the 8% of £15 and then to add this onto the £15

Percentage profit

If an article is bought at a cost price and then sold to make a profit, the percentage profit is the fractional increase multiplied by 100.

For example, Brian bought a Datsun for £250 and then the next day managed to sell it for £275. What was his percentage profit?

The profit was £275 – £250 which is £25; so the profit fraction is $\frac{25}{250}$. Multiply this by 100 to give 10%, so the percentage profit is 10%.

Exam Questions

1. Joy is given £250. She gives £75 of this to charity. What percentage is this of her share?
2. (a) In a survey of 3,600 adults, 68% said they were in favour of people carrying donor cards. Calculate the number of adults who said they were in favour.
   (b) In a particular region, only 140,000 adults carry donor cards. This is 5% of the adults in the region. Calculate the total number of adults in the region.

Solutions

1. $\frac{75}{250} \times 100 = 30\%$
2. (a) $3,600 \times 0.68 = 2,448$
   (b) $5\% = 140,000$
   $1\% = 140,000 \div 5 = 28,000$
   $100\% = 28,000 \times 100 = 2,800,000.$

CHECKPOINT

Can you:

(a) Find 5% of £115
(b) Decrease 450 g by 8%
(c) Express £5.40 as a % of £80

PERIMETER

The perimeter is the length of an outside edge of a plane shape. For example, the perimeter of a **rectangle** is all the four lengths added to each other. The perimeter of a **circle** is the circumference of that circle.

PERPENDICULAR

A **line** that is perpendicular to another line is at right angles to it. A **plane** that is perpendicular to another plane is at right angles to that plane.

Construct a perpendicular

Construction

PERSPECTIVE

The presenting of solid objects on a plane surface in such a way that they look like the *actual* objects viewed from particular points.

PI (π)

Pi is the ratio found when you divide the **circumference** of a circle by its **diameter**. Its presence has been known for a long time. However, its accuracy has troubled many mathematicians throughout history in that it is an **irrational number** and as such we cannot state it exactly.

Your calculator holds the value of pi to as accurate a level as you will need, and you are advised always to use the *calculator value of pi* whenever you need to use pi.

Examination questions will accept the use of **rounded** off values of pi, such as 3.14 or 3.142. When using any value of pi, do remember to round off to a suitable degree of accuracy.

Pi is used in particular in the following formulae:

- Circumference of circle = π × diameter of the circle
- Area of circle = π × square of the radius of the circle

PICTOGRAM

A pictogram is a display of information using pictures to represent the **frequency** like the table shown. It displays information with pictures. Here it displays the number of cups of tea drunk per week by Yorkshire bank managers in certain parts of Yorkshire.

Town	Daily tea intake
Dewsbury	🍵 🍵 🍵 🍵
Leeds	🍵 🍵 🍵
Barnsley	🍵 🍵 🍵 🍵 🍵
Wath	🍵 🍵 🍵

Key 🍵 = 10 cups of tea

Pictogram

Notice that the key is one cup of tea per 10 cups drunk; so we use half a cup of tea to represent 5 cups drunk.

This type of display can be effective and more interesting than other types of display of data. However, it tends to be rather less accurate; for example it would be difficult to represent one cup of tea on the pictogram shown.

PIECEWORK

Piecework is the system of payment based on paying for each piece of work done. This means that some people are paid purely for the amount of work they actually do. For example:

James is paid 17p for every component he assembles on his production line. In one day he managed to assemble 138 components. How much would he earn in a week if he was able to do this each day in a 5 day week?

He would earn £0.17 × 138 = £23.46; so in 5 days he would earn £23.46 × 5, which totals £117.30

PIE CHART

A pie chart is a circular picture which is divided into the ratio of the frequencies of the different events occurring, so called since it has the appearance of a pie. This pie chart illustrates the transport used by pupils of High Storres School one day. The actual information is difficult to read accurately, but it does show us that the vast majority of pupils at the school come by bus.

You are quite likely to be asked in an examination question to extract information from a pie chart.

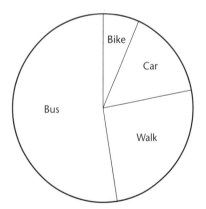

Pie chart

Constructing a pie chart

There is a set way to go about *constructing* a pie chart from given information. For example, suppose we are given the information in the table.

Church Expenditure	
Item	*Cost £*
Electric, gas	6,300
Minister wages and expenses	12,700
New Hymn books and Bibles	550
Posters and notices	280
Donations to other charities	3,800

We need to find the angle of the sector that each separate item will be. We do this by finding what fraction of the whole data each item is; we then use this to find the same fraction of a complete circle (i.e. of 360°).

> *Remember: If you are asked to draw a pie chart, always start by drawing the smallest angle first and finish by drawing the largest angle.*

The table below illustrates what we would do with the above information.

Item	Cost	Angle	
Electric/gas	6,300	$^{6300}/_{23630} \times 360 =$	96°
Minister	12,700	$^{12700}/_{23630} \times 360 =$	193°
Books	550	$^{550}/_{23630} \times 360 =$	8°
Posters etc	280	$^{280}/_{23630} \times 360 =$	4°
Donations	3,800	$^{3800}/_{23630} \times 360 =$	58°
Totals	23,630		359°

The table above and the second pie chart illustrate what we have done. Note how the angles in the chart have been rounded off to the nearest degree, so that their total is not exactly the 360° which you would normally expect to get. The pie chart was drawn smallest angle first, then next smallest, etc., until the largest one was drawn last of all. Drawing the largest angle last ensures that any slight error will be less noticeable.

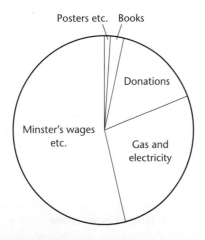

Note that although the pie charts you see in every day use will probably *not* have their sector angles labelled (e.g. 96°), this is usually expected in an examination question. In this case you are trying to show that you *know* what the angle should be.

Exam Question

Kevin spent £72
The table shows what he spent it on.

Items	Amount spent
Bus fares	£15
Going out	£21
Clothes	£18
CDs	£16
Other	£2
Total spending	£72

Kevin is asked to construct a pie chart to show his spending.
(a) Work out the angle of each sector of his pie chart.
(b) Draw accurately his pie chart.
(c) What percentage of Kevin's spending was on CDs?

Solution

(a) Kevin will need a final column where he works out his angles as

Items	Amount spent	Angles (in degrees)
Bus fares	£15	$\frac{15}{72} \times 360 = 75$
Going out	£21	$\frac{21}{72} \times 360 = 105$
Clothes	£18	$\frac{18}{72} \times 360 = 90$
CDs	£16	$\frac{16}{72} \times 360 = 80$
Other	£2	$\frac{2}{72} \times 360 = 10$
Total spending	£72	360

(b) You should have drawn a pie chart starting with the smallest angle first.
(c) $\frac{16}{72} \times 100 = 22.2\%$

Exam Question

The pie chart featuring a £1 coin is published by Dr Barnardo's in Northern Ireland to show how they spend each £1. If a school raised £2,680 for Dr Barnardo's:

(a) How much of that money would go directly to child care?
(b) How much would be spend on education and appeals?

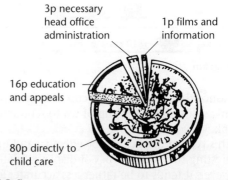

(NISEAC; I)

Solution

(a) $\dfrac{2680 \times 80}{100} = £2,144$

(b) $\dfrac{2680 \times 16}{100} = £428.80$

PLANE SHAPES

A plane shape is one that is two-dimensional; that is, it will have width and height but no depth.

You should recognize, be able to name, and know the distinguishing features between the following plane shapes:

● An *isosceles* triangle. This has two of its sides the same length and two angles the same. It will have a *line of symmetry* bisecting the angle included between the two equal sides.

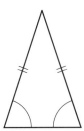

Isosceles triangle

● An *equilateral* triangle. This has all its three sides the same length and all its angles are 60°. Each angle bisector will bisect the opposite side and be a *line of symmetry*. It has *rotational symmetry* of order three.

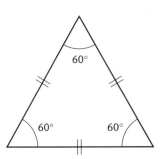

Equilateral triangle

● A *right-angled* triangle. This is one that contains a right angle.

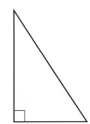

Right-angled triangle

● A *quadrilateral*. This has four sides, and the four angles it contains add up to 360°.

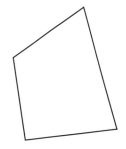

Quadrilateral

● A *square*. This has all four sides equal in length and each angle is 90°. It has four *lines of symmetry*, namely the two line bisectors and the two angle bisectors. It also has *rotational symmetry* of order four.

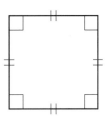

Square

● A *kite*. This is recognizable as a kite shape. It has four sides as shown; the top two sides are the same length and the bottom two sides are the same length. There is one *line of symmetry*, namely the line that bisects both angles included between the equal sides.

Kite

● A *parallelogram*. This has four sides and the opposite two sides are equal in length as well as being parallel. The angles *next to each other* will add up to 180° and the angles *opposite each other* will be equal. There is no *line of symmetry* but it does have *rotational symmetry* of order two.

Parallelogram

● A *rhombus*. This is a parallelogram that has all its sides the same length. Its diagonals are perpendicular, and bisect each other. There are two **lines of symmetry**, namely the angle bisectors. It has **rotational symmetry** of order two.

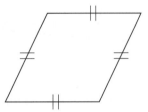

Rhombus

● A *trapezium*. This is a quadrilateral with a pair of opposite sides parallel. The pairs of angles between the parallel sides add up to 180°.

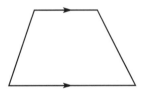

Trapezium

PLANS

The plan of a three-dimensional shape is the view you get when looking down from directly above the shape.

Some shapes and their plans are shown.

The most common mistake when asked to draw a plan is to draw a diagram that still has that three-dimensional look of *perspective* about it. You must be clear that a plan is a *two-dimensional view only* and it must have a two-dimensional appearance.

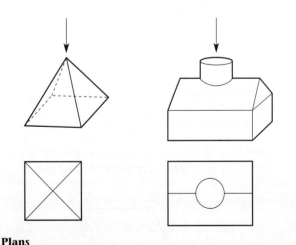

Plans

POINT SYMMETRY

Rotational symmetry

POLYGON

A polygon is a plane figure with many straight sides. The names of the ones you ought to know are:

● triangle   3 sides
● quadrilateral 4 sides
● pentagon   5 sides
● hexagon   6 sides
● septagon   7 sides
● octagon   8 sides
● nonagon   9 sides
● decagon   10 sides

Polygons have two main types of angle. There are interior angles and exterior angles (outside), as shown. A polygon has as many exterior angles as interior angles, which will be the same as the number of sides of the polygon:

● Exterior angles: all the exterior angles of any polygon will add up to 360°

● Interior angles: all the interior angles of an N-sided polygon add up to $180 \times (N-2)°$

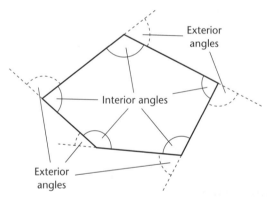

Polygons

Regular polygons

A regular polygon is one which has all its sides the same length and all its angles the same:

● *Exterior angle*: the exterior angle of a regular N-sided polygon is found by dividing 360° by N.

● *Interior angle*: the interior angle of a regular N-sided polygon can be found by either subtracting the exterior angle away from 180°, or by using the formula $\dfrac{180(N-2)°}{N}$

● Symmetry: an N-sided regular polygon has N **lines of symmetry** and **rotational symmetry** of order N.

Exam Question

A regular pentagon is inscribed in a circle of centre *O*.

(a) Prove that the total of all of the interior angles of the pentagon (at A, B, C, D and E) is 540°. Explain your reasoning.

(b) Calculate the size of angle ADB.

(NEAB; I)

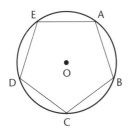

Solution

(a) Each exterior angle is $\frac{360}{5} = 72°$, hence each interior angle is $180 - 72 = 108$. So, the sum of all 5 interior angles is $108 \times 5 = 540°$.

(b) Consider the angle AOB; it will be $\frac{360}{5} = 72°$, then the angle ADB is half this, which is 36°

 Angles

```
CHECKPOINT

(a)  Calculate the exterior angle of a regular octagon.
(b)  Calculate the interior angle of a regular decagon.
```

POLYHEDRON/POLYHEDRA

A polyhedron is a solid figure bounded by plane polygonal faces. There are various types of polyhedra. For example, the *regular tetrahedron* has four equilateral triangular faces.

POSITION VECTORS

-+- *Vectors*

POWER

-+- *Exponent*

PREMIUM

A premium is an amount paid for an insurance or loan contract. You can have annual, monthly or even weekly premiums. For example, you can see from the loan table below that the premiums vary for different amounts required and for different types of loan (e.g. without or with protection insurance).

PRIME

A number is prime when it has exactly two **factors** which are itself and the number one. The first few prime numbers are 2, 3, 5, 7, 11, 13 and 17; as you see they all have only two factors. It should be noted that the number one is not a prime number as it has only one factor.

PRIME FACTOR

The prime factors of an **integer** are the factors that are prime numbers. For example, the prime factors of 33 are 3 and 11, which for convenience in this sense we write as 3×11. The prime factors of 18 are $2 \times 3 \times 3$ (note how we put the 3 down twice so that the product of these factors gives the integer we start with). You could check for yourself that the prime factors of 48 are $2 \times 2 \times 2 \times 2 \times 3$ which we would shorten to $2^4 \times 3$.

	12 MONTHLY REPAYMENTS APR 23.6%				
	Without protection insurance			*With protection insurance*	
Amount of loan £	*(Premium) monthly payment* £	*Total amount payable* £		*(Premium) monthly payment* £	*Total amount payable* £
500	46.66	559.92		47.87	574.44
600	56.00	672.00		57.49	689.88
700	65.33	783.96		67.01	804.12
800	74.66	895.92		76.62	919.44
900	84.00	1,008.00		86.24	1,034.88
1,000	93.33	1,119.96		95.75	1,149.00
1,100	102.66	1,231.92		105.36	1,264.32
1,200	112.00	1,344.00		114.98	1,379.76
1,300	121.33	1,455.96		124.50	1,494.00
1,400	130.66	1,567.92		134.11	1,609.32

CHECKPOINT

Write down all the Prime numbers greater than 20 but less than 50

PRISM

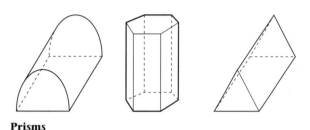

Prisms

A prism is a three-dimensional shape with a regular cross section through its height or its length. All the shapes shown are prisms, since they are shapes you could 'slice' up in such a way that each cross section would be identical.

The volume of any prism is found by multiplying the area of the regular cross section by its length (or height if it is stood on its regular cross section).

For example, the volume of the particular prism shown is the area of the triangular end multiplied by the length, which is: $\frac{1}{2} \times 5 \times 6 \times 8 = 120$ cm^3.

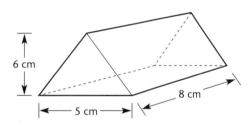

Remember: The regular cross section is the plane shape found at both ends of the prism.

Exam Question

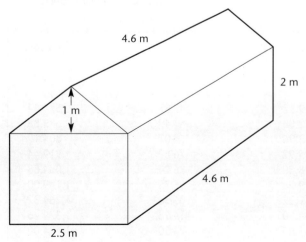

A greenhouse with the size and shape shown can be thought of as a cuboid with a triangular prism on top.

Mr Khan has built a greenhouse like this, and now wants a heater for it. To choose the right heater, he needs to know the volume of his greenhouse.

Calculate the volume of the greenhouse.

(NEAB; I)

Solution

The area of the end is a rectangle + a triangle, which is $(2 \times 2.5) + (\frac{1}{2} \times 2.5 \times 1) = 6.25$ m^2

So, the volume $= 6.25 \times 4.6 = 28.75$ m^3

PROBABILITY

The probability of an event happening is often given by a *fraction*:

$$\frac{\text{the number of ways the event can happen}}{\text{the total number of ways that equally likely events can happen}}$$

For example, the probability of cutting a pack of cards and getting an ace is $\frac{4}{52}$, since there are 4 possible aces to get and 52 equally likely cards to choose from.

There are three important probabilities to know:

● *No chance*: if an event is *impossible*, like rolling a normal dice and getting a nine, then the probability is 0

● *Even chance*: an event that we say has an *even chance*, like tossing a coin and getting a head, has a probability of $\frac{1}{2}$

● *Certainty*: if an event is *certain*, like rolling a dice and getting a number less than 7, then the probability is 1

So you can see, *all* probabilities lie somewhere between 0 and 1 inclusive. Of course:

● The smaller a fraction is, the less likely the event.

● The larger a fraction is, the more likely the event.

If the probability is given by a decimal, it can be changed into a fraction, e.g. $0.2 = \frac{2}{10}$

Note that you can write a probability as a:

● Fraction $\quad \frac{5}{8}$

● Decimal $\quad 0.7$

● Percentage $\quad 60\%$

But *never* express a probability as the following:

3 in 5, 4 out of 7, 2 : 3

You will *have* it marked wrong.

Combined events

When we want to find the probability of a *combined event* – that is, where two or more events are happening – then we need to be clear about whether we want two events to happen *at the same time* or whether either event can happen, but *not* at the same time. These two situations are types that can be described as AND and OR.

AND

AND is the type where both events do happen at the same time. To find this combined probability we *multiply* the probabilities of each single event.

> For example, what is the probability of rolling a normal dice twice and getting a three followed by an even number?

The probability of rolling a three is $\frac{1}{6}$
The probability of rolling an even number is $\frac{3}{6}$
Hence the combined probability is $\frac{1}{6} \times \frac{3}{6}$ which is $\frac{3}{36}$ which cancels down to $\frac{1}{12}$.

OR

OR is the type when either one event or the other can happen, but both cannot happen at the same time. To find this combined probability we *add* together their probabilities.

> For example, to win a game, Terry had to cut a pack of cards and get a king or the ace of spades. What is the probability of this happening?

The probability of cutting a king is $\frac{4}{52}$
The probability of cutting an ace of spades is $\frac{1}{52}$
Hence the combined probability is $\frac{4}{52} + \frac{1}{52}$ which is $\frac{5}{52}$

Exam Questions

1. The 400 children in a school each bought one ticket for the school prize draw. The 400 tickets, numbered 1 to 400, will be put into a barrel and the winning ticket drawn.

   (a) Mary has the ticket numbered 199.
       What is the probability that she will win the prize?
   (b) What is the probability that the winning ticket number will be smaller than 50?
   (c) Karl says 'Either a boy or a girl must win, so the probability that a girl will win is $\frac{1}{2}$.'
       Explain why he might be wrong.

2. (a) There are four socks in a drawer.

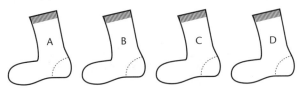

   (i) Two socks are chosen at random.
       One possible choice is A and B.
       Write down the other five possible choices.
   (ii) Two of the socks in the drawer are white and two are black. If two of the socks are chosen at random, what is the probability that a black pair will be chosen?
   (b) Another drawer contains red socks and green socks. The probability of choosing a red pair is 0.33. What is the probability that a red pair will *not* be chosen?

Solutions

1. (a) 1/400
   (b) 49/400
   (c) because the numbers of boys and girls might not be equal.
2. (a) (i) AC, AD, BC, BD and CD
       (ii) P(black sock) × P(black sock) = $\frac{2}{4} \times \frac{1}{3} = \frac{1}{6}$
   (b) 1 – 0.33 = 0.67

Tree diagrams

Tree diagrams are a very useful way of looking at all the possibilities of a given situation and they help us find various specific probabilities.
   For example, two twins, Helen and Neil, both swim for their country in an international competition. The coach quotes the probabilities of their getting gold medals as Helen 0.6 and Neil 0.7. What are the chances of both or either of them getting gold medals?
   We can illustrate the possibilities with a tree diagram, as shown. Notice how the individual probabilities have been put on the *branches* of the tree diagram, with each pair adding up to 1; this is because, for each pair, one of the branches *must* happen. Then to find the probabilities of the ***combined events*** you just multiply along the branches, as shown.

Helen	Neil	Result	Probability
	0.7 wins	both win	0.6 × 0.7 = 0.42
0.6 wins	0.3 loses	Helen only wins	0.6 × 0.3 = 0.18
0.4 loses	0.7 wins	Neil only wins	0.4 × 0.7 = 0.28
	0.3 loses	Neither win	0.4 × 0.3 = 0.12

Tree diagram

> Remember: The probabilities on a 'pair' of branches will always add up to 1.

✦ **Combined events**

Expectation

The expectation of any event happening is the probability of that event multiplied by the number of times the 'trial' is done.
   Suppose, for example, that the probability that any one light bulb manufactured by a certain firm is dud is 0.02. Then, if one day they produce 560 light bulbs, they *expect* to have 0.02 × 560 dud ones, which is 11.2 (round off to 11).

Exam Question

A bag contains five discs, identical in every way except that one is white and the other four are red. Two boys,

Alan and Ben, play a game whereby each takes it in turn to draw a disc at random from the bag without replacing it. The first one to draw the white disc is the winner. Given that Alan goes first, find the probability that:

(a) Alan wins at his first attempt,
(b) Ben wins at his first attempt,
(c) Ben wins.

(NEAB; H)

Solution
(a) $\frac{1}{5}$
(b) The probability is that Alan loses first *and* then Ben wins, which is $\frac{4}{5} \times \frac{1}{4} = \frac{1}{5}$
(c) For Ben to win, there are only two possibilities: Alan lose, Ben win, *or* Alan lose, Ben lose, Alan lose, Ben win. These chances will be $\frac{1}{5}$ or $\frac{4}{5} \times \frac{3}{4} \times \frac{2}{3} \times \frac{1}{2} = \frac{1}{5} + \frac{1}{5} = \frac{2}{5}$

CHECKPOINT

(a) What is the probability of being dealt an ace and then a king?
(b) What is the probability of being dealt two cards, one of them being an ace and the other one a king.

PROFIT

Profit is the amount of money gained by a transaction. It is usually calculated by subtracting cost price from selling price.

Percentage profit

Percentage profit is the profit divided by the cost price multiplied by 100 to turn the fraction into a percentage. For example, if a man bought a plant for 25p and then sold it for 40p, the profit is 15p, and his *percentage* profit is calculated as $\frac{15}{25} \times 100$ which is 60%.

PROPORTION

Proportion is the relation of one number with another to form a ratio. There are two types of proportion; direct and inverse. (This is a Higher Level topic only).

Direct proportion

Direct proportion is when there is a simple *multiplying* connection between two things. For example, if a spoon weighs 25 g, then the weight of any number of the same sized spoons is found by multiplying the number of spoons by 25 g. This is because the weight of the spoons is in direct proportion to their number.

This proportion, or **variation** as it is often called, is often related to the square or the cube of something. For example, the *volume of a sphere* is in direct proportion to the *cube of its radius*.

The alternative ways of saying that, for example, weight 'is directly proportional to' include the following:

● The weight *varies directly with* the number

● The weight $\propto$ the number

● The weight $= K \times$ (the number)

The last two are mathematically the most convenient to use and you could use this shorthand a lot. The K is a constant and is called the *constant of proportionality*.

For example, the mass of a ball bearing varies directly with the cube of the radius. A ball bearing with a radius of 3 cm has a mass of 450 g. Find the mass of a similar ball bearing with a radius of 2 cm. Since mass $\propto$ radius^3, then mass $= K \times R^3$ so when mass = 450 g and R = 3, then $450 = K \times 27$; hence $K = 16.666$

Therefore, when R = 2, then mass $= 16.666 \times 8 = 133.3$ g.

Inverse proportion

Inverse proportion is when there is a *dividing* connection between two things, so that as one increases the other decreases. For example, the more men involved in digging a hole, the quicker it will get dug (in theory anyway).

For example, the time taken to construct a building varies inversely with the square root of the number of people constructing it. If a building is constructed by 15 men in 28 days, how long will it take 21 people?
Since $T \propto 1/\sqrt{N}$ then $T = K/\sqrt{N}$
When T = 28, N = 15; hence $28 = K/\sqrt{15}$ and $K = 28 \times \sqrt{15}$
So when N = 21, $T = \dfrac{28 \times \sqrt{15}}{\sqrt{21}} = 23.66$ (call it 24 days).

Exam Question
A mathematician looking for Christmas presents noticed that three types of wine glass in a certain store were all similar in shape and that:

$$\frac{\text{radius of base of type A}}{\text{radius of base of type B}} = \frac{\text{radius of base of type B}}{\text{radius of base of type C}} = \frac{2}{3}$$

(a) Calculate:
(i) $\dfrac{\text{perimeter of bowl of glass type C}}{\text{perimeter of bowl of glass type B}}$

(ii) $\dfrac{\text{radius of base of glass type C}}{\text{radius of base of glass type A}}$

(iii) $\dfrac{\text{volume of bowl of glass type A}}{\text{volume of bowl of glass type B}}$

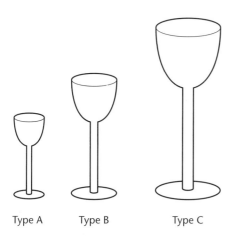

| Type A | Type B | Type C |

(b) If the prices of the wine glasses were in direct proportion to the volume of bowl, and glass type B cost £3.51, what would be the price of glass type A?

(NEAB, H)

Solution

(a) (i) $\frac{3}{2}$; (ii) $(\frac{3}{2})^2 = \frac{9}{4}$; (iii) $(\frac{2}{3})^3 = \frac{8}{27}$

(b) £3.51 × $\frac{8}{27}$ = £1.04

PYRAMID

A pyramid can have any shape for its base. But from each point on the perimeter of the base there is a straight line going up to the top and all these lines will meet at one point, called the *vertex*. The illustration shows a square-based pyramid (often the name of the pyramid will reflect the shape of the base).

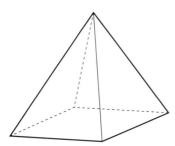

Square-based pyramid

A pyramid with a circular base, however, is called a **cone**. When the vertex of a pyramid is vertically above the centre of the base, the correct name is a 'right pyramid'.

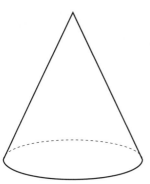

Cone (circular-based pyramid)

The volume of any pyramid is found by multiplying its base area by one third of its height:

volume = base area × $\frac{1}{3}$ height

Exam Question

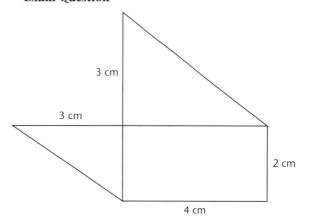

The diagram is part of a net of a pyramid with a rectangular base.

(a) Draw accurately the complete net.
(b) Using the dimensions shown on the diagram, calculate the total surface area of the pyramid.

Solution

(a) We see that the two missing sides also need to be right-angled triangles, with heights equal to the diagonals of the adjacent triangles. You can find these lengths by using a pair of compasses.

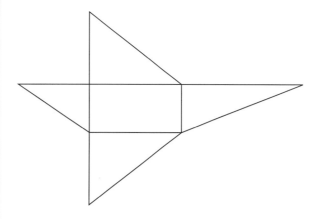

(b) The area of the rectangle and two triangles shown in the first diagram are;

$(2 × 4) + (\frac{1}{2} × 4 × 3) + (\frac{1}{2} × 2 × 3) = 17$ cm^2

We can calculate the heights of the two extra triangles on the net by Pythagoras:

right-hand side triangle height = $\sqrt{(3^2 + 4^2)}$ = 5 cm
bottom triangle height = $\sqrt{(2^2 + 3^2)}$ = 3.6 cm
So the area of these two triangles will be

$(\frac{1}{2} × 2 × 5) + (\frac{1}{2} × 4 × 3.6) = 12.2$ cm^2

So the whole surface area will be 12.2 + 17 = 29.2 cm^2

PYTHAGORAS

Pythagoras was a Greek mathematician who later lived in South Italy in the latter half of the sixth century BC. He organized many groups of scholars to probe into geometry, philosophy, religion and politics.

Pythagoras' theorem

Many researchers now believe that it was *not* Pythagoras who first *discovered* this theorem, although it is quite likely that Pythagoras did, in his own time, find it out for himself. The theorem states that:

'In a right-angled triangle, the sum of the squares of the two smaller sides is equal to the square of the longest side.'

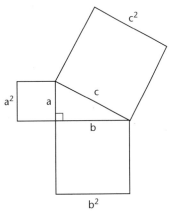

Pythagoras' theorem

> *Remember: In a Pythagoras problem, you will have to find a square root to get your final answer. Round off to give one more significant figure than the starting figures.*

In other words, looking at the triangle in the figure above, with sides a, b and c:

$$a^2 + b^2 = c^2$$

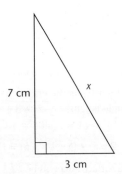

You need to be able to use the formula to find missing sides in right-angled triangles when you know the other two sides.

For example, in the previous figure, to find x, use Pythagoras' theorem to state that $x^2 = 3^2 + 7^2 = 9 + 49 = 58$; hence $x = \sqrt{58} = 7.6$ cm.

In the figure below, to find y use Pythagoras' theorem to state $y^2 = 11^2 - 6^2 = 121 - 36 = 85$; hence $y = \sqrt{85} = 9.22$ cm.

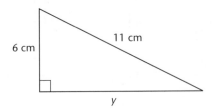

Three-dimension Pythagoras' theorem

The theorem of Pythagoras extends into *three dimensions*. In a cuboid of dimension *a* by *b* by *c* the length of the diagonal from one corner to the opposite corner is found by square rooting the sum of the squares of the dimensions. In other words:

length of diagonal = $\sqrt{(a^2 + b^2 + c^2)}$

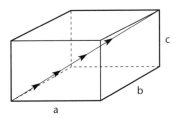

Three-dimensional Pythagoras' theorem

Exam Question

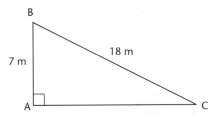

ABC is a right-angled triangle.
AB is of length 7 m and BC is of length 18 m.

(a) Calculate the length of AC.
(b) Calculate the size of angle ABC.

Solution
(a) AC = $\sqrt{(18^2 - 7^2)}$ = 16.6 m² (rounded)
(b) cos B = $\frac{7}{18}$ = 0.3888 the angle with a cosine of 0.3888 is 67.1°.

CHECKPOINT

A right-angled triangle has one side 5 cm another side 4 cm.

Calculate the two different possible lengths of the other side.

QUADRATIC

A quadratic is an expression that involves powers of two, but none higher than 2; for example $x^2 + 5x - 9$.

Quadratic expansion

When we have an expression such as $(2x + 3)(3x - 4)$ it can be **expanded** and a quadratic expression can clearly be seen.

It is the *multiplying out* of such pairs of brackets that is usually called a quadratic expansion.

The rule for expanding such expressions as $(x + 4)(3x - 5)$ is similar to expanding single brackets:

'multiply everything in one bracket with everything in the other bracket'.

Example 1

$(x + 3)(x + 5) = x^2 + 5x + 3x + 15$
$= x^2 + 8x + 15$

Example 2

$(t + 4)(t - 1) = t^2 - t + 4t - 4$
$= t^2 + 3t - 4$

Example 3

$(w - 3)(w - 2) = w^2 - 2w - 3w + 6$
$= w^2 - 5w + 6$

Quadratic factorization

This is putting the quadratic expression back into its brackets (if possible). The type of quadratic you will need to be able to factorize in the Intermediate GCSE examinations are the type:

$$x^2 + ax + b$$

where a and b are integers. There are some simple rules that can be applied that will enable you to have a logical way of trying to factorize these expressions.

Rules

- The signs start off your brackets

  i.e. $x^2 + ax + b = (x + ?)(x + ?)$ since all signs are positive
  $x^2 - ax + b = (x - ?)(x - ?)$ since $-ve \times -ve = +ve$ for the last sign

So if the *last* sign is a plus both signs in the brackets are the same as the *first* sign. And if the *last* sign is a

minus then the two signs in brackets will be different.

$x^2 + ax - b = (x + ?)(x - ?)$
$x^2 - ax - b = (x + ?)(x - ?)$ since $+ve \times -ve = -ve$

- Now look at the last number (the b):
  The two *end* numbers of the brackets have to multiply together to give this number.

- Now look at the middle number (the a):

  If *both* your bracket signs are the *same* then you are looking for the two end numbers of your brackets to *add* up to this number.

  If *both* the bracket signs are *different* then you are looking for the two end numbers to have a *difference* of this number.

Follow through these examples to see how straightforward this is.

Example 1
Factorize $x^2 + 6x + 8$.

Solution
We note both brackets start with an x, so

$$(x \quad)(x \quad)$$

We see that the last sign is positive, hence both bracket signs will be the same as the first, which is plus, so

$$(x + \quad)(x + \quad)$$

We note the end bracket numbers multiply together to give 8:

i.e. 1,8 or 2,4

We note the signs in the brackets are the same so the end bracket numbers must add up to 6, the middle number, hence this must be the 2,4 choice.

So the brackets become

$$(x + 2)(x + 4)$$

This can be expanded out if you wish to convince yourself that it has worked.

Example 2
Factorize $x^2 - 7x + 12$.

Solution
We note both brackets start with an x, so

$$(x \quad)(x \quad)$$

We see that the last sign is positive, so both bracket signs will be the same as the first, which is minus, so

$$(x - \quad)(x - \quad)$$

We note that the end bracket numbers multiply together to give 12:

i.e. 1,12 or 2,6 or 3,4

We note the signs in the brackets are the same so the end bracket numbers must add up to 7, the middle number, hence this must be the 3,4 choice.

So the brackets become

$$(x - 3)(x - 4)$$

This can be expanded out if you wish to convince yourself that it has worked.

Example 3
Factorize $t^2 + 5t - 6$.

Solution
We note both brackets start with a t, so

$$(t \quad)(t \quad)$$

We see that the last sign is negative, hence both bracket signs will be different, so

$$(t + \quad)(t - \quad)$$

We note that the end bracket numbers multiply together to give 6:

i.e. 1,6 or 2,3

We note that the signs are *different* so the end bracket numbers will have a *difference* of 5, hence this must be the 1,6 choice.

We now have to decide which number goes with the negative and which with the positive. Since the middle term of $5t$ is *positive* we need *more* positives than negatives, hence the bigger number goes with the positive.

So the brackets become

$$(t + 6)(t - 1)$$

This can be expanded out if you wish to convince yourself that it has worked.

Example 4
Factorize $x^2 - 6x - 16$.

Solution
We note both brackets start with an x, so

$$(x \quad)(x \quad)$$

We see that the last sign is negative, hence both bracket signs will be different:

$$(x + \quad)(x - \quad)$$

We note that the end bracket numbers multiply together to give 16:

i.e. 1,16 or 2,8 or 4,4

We note that since the signs are *different* the end bracket numbers will have a *difference* of 6, hence this must be the 2,8 choice.

We now have to decide which number goes with the negative and which with the positive. Since the middle term of $6x$ is *negative* we need *more* negatives than positives, hence the bigger number goes with the negative.

So the brackets become

$$(x + 2)(x - 8)$$

This can be expanded out if you wish to convince yourself that it has worked.

Example 5 (the difference of two squares)
Factorize $x^2 - 25$.

Solution
If we write this as $x^2 + 0x - 25$ it will help us to see a pattern.

We note the brackets start with an x, so,

$$(x \quad)(x \quad)$$

We see that the last sign is negative, so the signs in the brackets will be *different*, so

$$(x + \quad)(x - \quad)$$

We see the *difference* between the end numbers is 0, so they must be the same.

We see that the end numbers multiply to give 25, they need to be the same, so the end numbers must both be 5.

So the brackets become

$$(x + 5)(x - 5)$$

Factorizing expressions of the form $ax^2 + bx + c$

At the Higher Level of GCSE you need to be able to factorize these.

This follows a similar routine to that for factorizing $x^2 + ax + b$, but we now have the added complication of the factors of the coefficient of x^2.

Follow through the following examples to see how we can cope with this.

Example 1
Factorize $2x^2 + 11x + 12$

Solution
Both signs are positive, so the bracket signs are both positive, so

$$(\quad + \quad)(\quad + \quad)$$

The 2 has only one pair of factors, 2×1, so can easily be placed as $(2x + \quad)(x + \quad)$.

The 12 has three possible factor pairs 12×1, 2×6 and 3×4

We now look at a combination of the 2×1 and the factors of 12 to look for a pair that will combine to give 11;

$$2 \mid 12 \quad 2 \quad 3$$
$$1 \mid 1 \quad 6 \quad 4$$

We will see that the combination of 2×4 and 1×3 will *add up* to 11.

So, the complete factorization becomes $(2x + 3)(x + 4)$

Example 2
Factorize $12x^2 - 19x + 4$.

Solution
The last sign is positive, so both signs in the brackets are the same as the first sign in the expression. So both signs are negative in the brackets, so

$$(\quad - \quad)(\quad - \quad)$$

The 12 has three factor pairs, 4 has just the two. We need a combination that adds up to 19:

$$12 \quad 6 \quad 4 \mid 4 \quad 2$$
$$1 \quad 2 \quad 3 \mid 1 \quad 2$$

We see that the combination 3×1 and 4×4 will *add up* to 19.

So, the complete factorization is $(3x - 4)(4x - 1)$. Notice from the combination of factor pair where each number has to go in the brackets to be able to multiply to the correct expression.

Example 3
Factorize $6x^2 - x - 15$

Solution
The last sign is negative, so the signs in the brackets are different $(\ +\ )(\ -\ )$.

The 6 has two factor pairs, as does the 15, but because the signs are different, we want a *difference* of 1 to be made:

$$
\begin{array}{cc|cc}
6 & 3 & 3 & 15 \\
1 & 2 & 5 & 1
\end{array}
$$

We see that the combination 2×5 and 3×3 will give a difference of 1, and since the 1 is a negative number, we need the larger combination to be negative in the brackets:

$$(2x + 3)(3x - 5).$$

Difference of two squares

If you expand $(x + y)(x - y)$ in the normal way you get the quadratic $x^2 - y^2$. This is called the difference of two squares; it is very useful to recognize when this is present, especially when we wish to **factorize**. The situation is recognizable as being the subtraction of two expressions that can be square rooted quite easily.

For example, to solve $9x^2 - 16 = 0$, we recognize a difference of two squares.

This gives us $(3x + 4)(3x - 4) = 0$

hence $x = -\frac{4}{3}$ and $\frac{4}{3}$

Graphs of quadratic equations

If the equation is of a quadratic nature, i.e. $y = ax^2 + bx + c$, then it will be a $\cup$-shaped curve if a is positive, and a $\cap$-shaped curve if a is negative. The value of c is the y-axis intercept.

For example, look at this sketch of the graph of $y = 3x^2 + 2x - 1$.

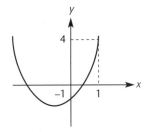

Since the a is positive we know it's a $\cup$-shape, since the c is –1 we know it cuts through the y-axis at $y = -1$, and when $x = 1$, $y = 3 + 2 - 1$ which is 4. Hence a sketch could look like that shown.

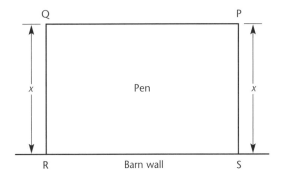

Exam Question
A farmer has 16 m of fencing which he is going to use to make a rectangular pen PQRS in which to keep chickens.

He has been advised that he should allow 1 m^2 for each chicken. The pen is to be built using a barn wall as one side, as shown. He wants to design the pen in such a way that he can keep the maximum number of chickens in it.

Let the length of *PS* be x metres.

(a) Write down, in terms of x, an expression for the length of the side *PQ*.
(b) Show that the area, A square metres, of the pen is given by $A = 2x(8 - x)$.
(c) Complete the table below, which gives the value of A for different possible values of x.

x	0	1	2	3	3.5	4	4.5	5	6	7	8
A		14	24	30	31.5			30	24	14	0

(d) Draw the graph of A against x. Use your graph to find the maximum number of chickens that the farmer may keep in the pen and calculate the dimensions of the pen that he should use.

(NEAB; H)

Solution
(a) PQ = $16 - 2x$
(b) Area = $x(16 - 2x)$
   $= 16x - 2x^2 = 2x(8 - x)$
(c)

x	0	4	4.5
Area	0	32	31.5

(d) The graph will be a $\cap$-shape from (0,0) to (8,0).
   maximum chickens (area) = 32
   dimension of pen = 4×8 m.

CHECKPOINT

(a) Expand and simplify $(2x + 5)(3x - 4)$
(b) Factorize $x^2 + 3x - 10$

QUADRILATERAL

A quadrilateral is a four-sided plane figure. Its inside angles add up to 360°.

Cyclic quadrilateral

Any quadrilateral drawn so that its four vertices touch the circumference of a circle is said to be *cyclic*. Its opposite angles will add up to 180°. For example, in the figure below $(a + c) = (b + d) = 180°$. It is also true that any quadrilateral that has opposite side angles adding up to 180° is cyclic and hence a circle can be drawn around the vertices.

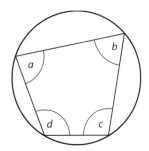

Cyclic quadrilateral

QUARTILE

Quartiles are found by dividing a **cumulative frequency** (c.f.) into four quarters. The points on the c.f. that give us the quartiles can be found by dividing the total frequency into four equal groups.

As you see on the diagram of a c.f., we actually have three quartiles. The lowest line gives us the lower quartile; the middle line gives us the median; and the highest line gives us the upper quartile.

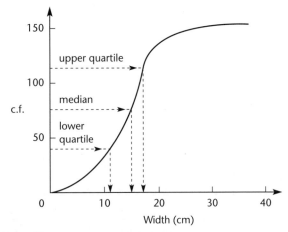

Quartile

In general to find the quartiles of a distribution of a frequency N:
● The lower quartile is found at $(N + 1)/4$ on the c.f.

● The median is found at $(N + 1)/2$ on the c.f.

● The upper quartile is found at $3 \times (N + 1)/4$ on the c.f.

Interquartile range

The interquartile range is the numeric difference between the upper quartile and the lower quartile. For example, in the case in question, the upper quartile is 16.6 and the lower quartile is 11.2, so the interquartile range is 16.6 – 11.2 = 5.4

> *Remember: The interquartile range gives you the ranges of the middle 50% of the population.*

Semi-interquartile range

This is exactly what it says: half of the interquartile range. In our example, the semi-interquartile range is $\frac{5.4}{2} = 2.7$

QUESTIONNAIRES

When asking questions on a questionnaire you have to be careful to note the following points:

● Never ask leading questions designed to get a particular response.

● Never ask personal irrelevant questions.

● Always keep the questions as simple as possible.

● Always set a question that will get a response from whoever is asked.

The following types of question are *bad questions* and should not appear on any of your questionnaires:

'How old are you?', This is personal, many will not want to answer.

'Murdering small lambs for food is cruel to the poor defensive animals, don't you agree?' This is a leading question, designed to get a 'yes'.

'Do you drink tea when abroad?' This can only be answered by those people who have been abroad.

'When shopping do you look for a space to park your car close to where you want to shop, or do you look for a car park or do you just park in the first space you see?' This is a rather complicated question.

The following types of questions are good questions in contrast to the poor ones above.

Which age group are you   0–20
                                       21–30
                                        31–40
                                        41–50
                                        over 50

'Do you think it is right to kill animals for meat to feed humans?'

'If you went abroad would you drink tea?'

'Do you look for a car-parking space close to where you want to shop?'

A questionnaire is usually put together to test a **hypothesis** or a statement made by someone.

For example:

'People don't use greengrocers any more, they buy vegetables from a supermarket because they can choose their own.'

Design a questionnaire that can be used to test if this statement is true or not.

The questions we need to include are:

- 'Do you regularly buy vegetables from the supermarket?'

- 'Do you regularly buy vegetables from a greengrocer?'

- 'Do you like to choose your own vegetables?'

Once these questions have been answered they can be looked at to see if the majority of people held similar views to that of the statement or not.

Exam Question

This cutting was taken from a local newspaper.

> The under 40s will often go to discos while abroad, but the over 40s will not even go to a disco in their own town!

Design a questionnaire you could use to see if the statement is true.

Solution

Which age group are you in?	40 or over ☐
	under 40 ☐
Do you go abroad?	yes ☐
	no ☐
Do you go to Discos in your own town?	yes ☐
	no ☐
Would you go to a disco if you were abroad?	yes ☐
	no ☐

RADIUS

The radius of a circle is the distance from the centre of the circle to the **circumference**. It is exactly half of the **diameter** of a circle.

RANGE

The range of a set of data is simply the difference between the highest and the lowest value. For example, in a set of data about heights of pupils, Sean was the tallest with 195 cm and Simon was the smallest with 98 cm. The range is 195–98, which gives us 97 cm.

RATE

A rate is a fixed ratio between two things. The idea of 'rate' is used quite a lot; e.g. speed, which is the rate of distance travelled per unit of time, or costs of hiring items, say a boat at the rate of £1.50 per hour.

The gradient of a graph will usually give you a rate of some sort connected with the units. For example, the gradient of a distance/time graph gives you the rate of change of distance, which is **speed**; and the gradient of a velocity/time graph gives you the rate of change of velocity, which is **acceleration**.

> *Remember: You will find the units of the rate from the units of the information, e.g. grams per cm³, metres per second.*

Speed

This is an important rate you should be familiar with; it is the rate of change of distance. It is useful to know that:

$$\text{speed} = \frac{\text{distance travelled}}{\text{time taken}}$$

Exchange rates

✦ *Exchange rates*

Exam Question

(a) Margaret and David want to find out how much petrol their car uses in miles per gallon. They fill the car with petrol when the reading on the milometer is:

0 2 8 3 4 0

After a few days they stop at a garage selling petrol at £1.70 per gallon. They fill the car up again and the cost of the petrol is £13.60.
By this time the milometer reading is:

0 2 8 6 2 0

How many miles per gallon does the car do over this period?

(WJEC; I)

(b) According to the *Guinness Book of Records*, the steepest temperature rise ever recorded occurred in South Dakota on 22 January 1943 when the temperature rose from –20 °C at 7.30 a.m. to 7.2 °C at 7.32 a.m.
   (i) By how much did the temperature rise?
   (ii) What was the average rate at which the temperature was rising in °C/s?

(NEAB; I)

Solution
(a) The distance covered is 280 miles, the petrol used is 8 gallons, hence the miles per gallon is 280 ÷ 8, which is 35 mpg.
(b) (i) 7.2 °C – –20 °C = 27.2 °C
    (ii) 7.2 °C per 2 minutes, i.e. 120 seconds. hence 27.2 ÷ 120 = 0.227 °C/s.

RATIO

Ratio is a comparison between two (or more) amounts, often written with 'to' or a colon (:). Many mathematical problems are sorted out by the formal use of ratio.

A ratio such as 12:8 can be simplified (or cancelled down) in a similar way to fractions, by dividing both sides by the same amount. Here 12:8 can be simplified to 3:2

For example, a good blend of tea can be made from Gunpowder tea and Lapsang in the ratio of 5:3. How much of each tea is there in a 500 g packet?

Add together the parts of the ratio to get 8, and then divide this into 500 g to get 62.5 g. Multiply this amount by the two individual parts of the ratio to give:

Gunpowder tea   5 × 62.5 g = 312.5 g *and*
Lapsang tea   3 × 62.5 g = 187.5 g

Exam Question
Here is a recipe for making 16 biscuits.

> **LEMON BUTTER BISCUITS**
> 6 oz Butter
> 2 oz Icing sugar
> 1/2 teaspoon Vanilla essence
> 1 Lemon, finely grated
> 4 oz Plain flour
> 2 oz Cornflour
> 1 Egg, beaten

(a) How many biscuits can be made using 12 oz of plain flour if there is enough of all the other ingredients available?

(b) How much plain flour is needed for 24 biscuits?

(NEAB; F)

Solutions
(a) $12 \div 4 = 3$; hence three lots of 16 can be made, which is 48
(b) 4 oz are used for 16 biscuits
so 1 oz is used for 4 biscuits
hence 6 oz will be needed for 24 biscuits.

Exam Question
Three ice hockey players score 12, 11 and 7 goals respectively. Their club pays out £4,500 in bonus money to these players. They share the bonus in the same ratio as the goals they score. Calculate the share of the bonus for each player.

Solution
Total number of 'shares' $12 + 11 + 7 = 30$
One share will equal $£4,500 \div 30 = £150$
12 shares = $£150 \times 12 = £1,800$
11 shares = $£150 \times 11 = £1,650$
7 shares = $£150 \times 7 = £1,050$

CHECKPOINT

Two shapes are similar. Their length ratios are 3:4.

Write down their:

(a) Area ratio.
(b) Volume ratio.

RATIONAL

A rational number is one which can be expressed as a vulgar fraction, i.e. as a/b, where both a and b are integers. A rational number is always either a **terminating decimal** or a **recurring decimal**.
(This is a high level topic only.)

Irrational

Any number that is not rational is irrational. The two most quoted irrational numbers are π and $\sqrt{2}$

CHECKPOINT

Write down an irrational number between 4 and 5

REAL NUMBER

A real number is one that is either **rational** or **irrational**. All the possible numbers that you can come across in a GCSE course are real numbers. To find out about numbers that are *not* real then you

need to study A level mathematics, where for instance you can find out about *imaginary* numbers.

RECIPROCAL

The reciprocal of a number is the result of dividing that number into 1. For example the reciprocal of 5 is $\frac{1}{5}$

The reciprocal of any **vulgar fraction** is that vulgar fraction turned upside down; for example the reciprocal of $\frac{3}{4}$ is $\frac{4}{3}$

On many calculators there is a button that calculates reciprocals for you, you will recognize it as $\boxed{\frac{1}{x}}$

Reciprocal equations

✥ *Equations, Graphs*

RECTANGLE

A rectangle is a four-sided, plane shape where the opposite sides are parallel as well as being of the same length. All the angles of a rectangle are right angles. It has two **lines of symmetry**, namely each line bisector, and it has **rotational symmetry** of order two.

The area of a rectangle is found by multiplying the base length by the height.

RECTANGULAR BLOCK

✥ *Cuboid*

RECURRING

✥ *Decimal*

REFLECTION

A mathematical reflection is the mirror image of a shape drawn on the opposite side of a mirror line, such that each line drawn from one point to its reflection is perpendicular to the mirror line.

When asked to draw a reflection of a shape in a given line, there are two ways of doing it:

1. If you were asked to reflect the triangle ABC in the line XY, you could use the following steps:

● Trace the figure ABC as well as the mirror line XY.

● Then, flip the tracing over, so that the figure ABC appears to the right of the line XY with the traced line XY exactly on top of the original XY (make sure the X is on top of X and the Y on top of Y).

● Then, with a pencil, press down on the vertices of the triangle to make a 'dint' in the paper underneath.

● Take the tracing paper away and join up the dots; this will give you the reflection. Do this carefully and it is a very good way.

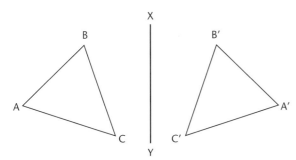

Reflection

2. The other way is to draw faint lines from each vertex of the triangle perpendicular to the line XY and to extend each line the other side of XY. Make lines the same distance either side of the mirror line, and the end points of the lines can be joined up to give you the reflected shape. If this is done on squared paper, as many in an examination are, then this method is the most accurate.

> *Remember: The mirror line is a **line of symmetry** between a shape and its reflection.*

The most common mistake made in reflections is to draw the same shape on the opposite side of the mirror line but either too near or too far away, and to get the 'line of symmetry' wrong, so that the reflection ends up also being translated.

Exam Question

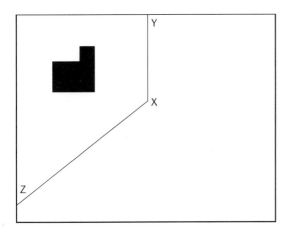

A plot of land has a house (shaded in the diagram) built on it. The builder wants to build two more houses. One house is to be the reflection of the existing house in the

fence XY and the other is to be the reflection of the existing house in the fence XZ.

(a) In the diagram, show the positions of the two new houses.
(b) What type of transformation would map the two reflections onto each other?

(NEAB; I)

Solution
(a) See diagram.

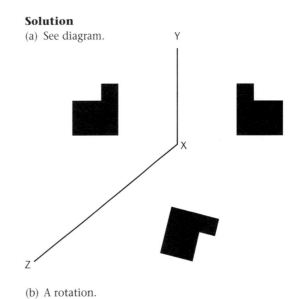

(b) A rotation.

RHOMBUS

A rhombus is a special **parallelogram** that has all its sides the same length. Its diagonals bisect each other at right angles and are **lines of symmetry**. It still has **rotational symmetry** of order two.

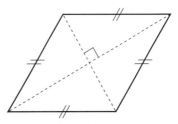

> *Remember: The area of a rhombus can be found by multiplying the lengths of both diagonals and halving the result.*

RIGHT ANGLE

A right angle is a quarter turn, which is 90°.

Right-angled triangles

The solution of right-angled triangles, that is finding lengths and angles, can be done by **trigonometry** and **Pythagoras**.

ROTATION

A *rotation* is a turn about some point. In mathematics, a rotation is meant as the process which transforms a shape to a different position by turning it around some point, called the *centre of rotation*, through a particular angle.

For the GCSE examinations you need to be able to rotate through multiples of 90°.

One way to do rotations is to use tracing paper:

- Trace the shape you wish to rotate, with the centre of rotation marked suitably with a cross indicating the lines of the grid you're rotating on.

- Then, with your pencil-point on the centre of rotation, turn the tracing paper until you see that the lines at the centre of rotation have moved through the angle you wish.

- Now press through each vertex of the shape with your pencil.

- Take away the tracing paper and join up the dots you have just made.

The shape produced in this way should be the same size as the original, but in a different position.

> Remember: In your GCSE examination, the rotations will be around the origin.

When you have practised quite a few rotations you should be able to draw them without having to trace each time but simply by thinking through where the shape is going to rotate to.

The most common mistake is to get the wrong centre of rotation. In most cases the centre of rotation is likely to be the origin, but not necessarily so. So do be careful to look for where the centre of rotation actually is, and not where you might want to see it!

ROTATIONAL SYMMETRY

 Symmetry

ROUNDING

Rounding off is the process by which we make approximate answers to a problem. It helps in presenting an answer to a sensible degree of accuracy. It is essential that you can round off properly, as it is a situation that will crop up in your examinations quite often.

To round off to a specific **decimal place** or **significant figure**, the rules are basically the same:

> Remember: You should not leave an answer with a lot of decimal places unless the question has asked you to.
> Always look to round off your answer and then see if the answer looks sensible.

- Decide where you need to round off to; perhaps one decimal place or two significant figures or the nearest ten. If in doubt, use one more significant figure than has been used in the question.

- Then look at the *next* digit:

  If it's less than a 5, you round down.
  If it's 5 or bigger, you round up.

For example:

32.547...	rounds to 32.5	to one decimal place
	rounds to 33	to the nearest whole number
0.0964...	rounds to 0.1	to one significant figure
	rounds to 0.10	to two decimal places
34,729...	rounds to 35,000	to the nearest thousand
	rounds to 30,000	to one significant figure

The most common error is one which some calculators do, namely to cut short the final answer; in other words to just chop off the bits beyond what's wanted, instead of rounding off.

Also some candidates make problems for themselves by rounding off too soon; try not to round off until the final answer in a problem. Otherwise the earlier rounding off may make your final answer inaccurate.

CHECKPOINT

Round off 3,198.573

(a) To two significant figures.
(b) To the nearest whole number.
(c) To one decimal place.

SALARIES

Salaries are the amounts of money people earn in a year. They are usually paid in either 12 monthly payments throughout the year, or 13 payments every four weeks. If an examination question refers to someone being paid monthly, you should assume that it is *calendar months* they are being paid (that is 12 payments per year) and not *lunar months* (that is 13 payments a year). If it is the lunar month payment, then the question will say so.

SCALE

Using scales

Scale is 1 : 800,000

Scale of a map

Maps have scales which are usually written down as a **ratio**; for example 1:1,000 would mean that every 1 cm on the map would represent 1,000 cm in reality (which is 10 metres).

For example, the scale on the map is 1:800,000

Scale drawings

In the same way that a scale on a map is written as a **ratio**, we can use the same principle for buildings, say designing a house.

For example, on a *scale drawing* a scale of 1:100 would mean that every 1 cm on the house plan would represent 100 cm in the house.

Exam Question

Mr and Mrs Johnston decided to join two rooms by removing part of the wall to form an archway. They sent a rough sketch to the builder who made an accurate scale drawing. Using the information in the sketch, construct a scale diagram using the scale 1:20.

(NISEAC; I)

Solution

Look at the figure. You should convert the given units to cm, then divide each by 20 to find the lengths to use. Construct each right angle from the base line, find the centre, then use a pair of compasses to draw the semi-circle.

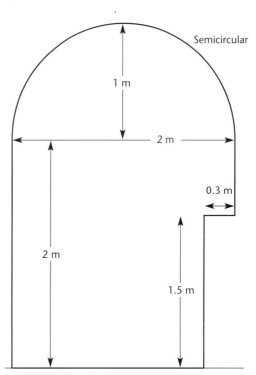

Scale factor

A scale factor is the multiplying factor of an **enlargement**. Each original length is multiplied by the scale factor to find the new length.

Models also often have scale factors; for example the model railways 00 gauge is made on a scale of 1:100

Scale of a graph

The scale of a graph is the relationship between the squares on the axes and the numbers they represent. Often, in examination questions, the scale is given to you; for example on the horizontal axis use a scale of 1 cm to 20 g.

If you are faced with having to *choose* your own scale, then remember, the bigger the scale – the more accurate is the graph. But also remember that there is a limit on the size of your graph paper.

You need to look at the *largest number* that you need to put onto each axis and then to see how best this fits in with the squares available on the paper. Take care to choose a scale that will help you to easily work out the position of the in-between numbers. For example, a scale going up in 3s, 4s or 7s etc. is no good since you cannot easily determine the numbers in between. Your scale should go up in 2s, 5s, 10s, 20s, etc. When you have decided on the scale of your graph then do remember to fully *label* the axes; for example, time (seconds), distance (metres), or price (£), etc. Do not forget the *units* of the labels; these are important, you could lose marks if they are not there.

SCATTER DIAGRAMS

A scatter diagram is one which plots quite a few points representing *two* factors or *variables*. For example, people's different weight with their height; or age with their pocket money. The scatter diagram will help you see if there is any relationship between the two factors.

Name	Height	Weight
James	160 cm	64 kg
John	150	45
Joseph	80	19
Paul	150	44
Michael	145	37
Jenny	100	21
Robert	160	56
Helen	165	61
Neil	165	65
Kirsty	130	33
Gary	180	69
Mark	175	70

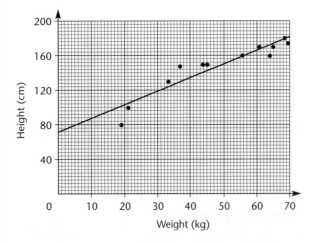

For example, we have scattered the information about some children's heights and weights on the diagram shown. Each child is represented by a blob which is a co-ordinate found from (weight, height). From the chart we can deduce that the taller the child, the heavier the child. But further than that we can, from the **line of best fit** that has been drawn, estimate the 'normal weight' for any child, given their height.

This line of best fit should be a straight line, unless the data is such that it shows an obvious curve that you can follow.

> Remember: A line of best fit does **not** necessarily simply go from the first point to the last. Nor does it have to start at the origin. Make sure it illustrates the trend of the data.

Exam Question

Ten people entered a craft competition. Their displays of work were awarded marks by two different judges

Competitor	A	B	C	D	E	F	G	H	I	J
First judge	90	35	60	15	95	25	5	100	70	45
Second judge	75	30	55	20	75	30	10	85	65	40

The table shows the marks that the two judges gave to each of the competitors.

(a) Draw a scatter diagram to show this information, and on your diagram draw a line of best fit.
(b) A late entry was given 75 marks by the first judge. Use your scatter diagram to estimate the mark that might have been given by the second judge. (Show how you found your answer)

Solution

(a) The diagram with a line of best fit should look like this;

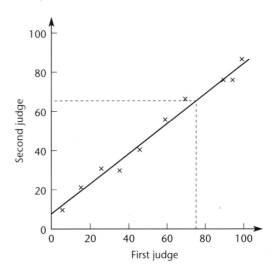

(b) The line used to find the second Judges score is shown on the above diagram. Follow the line from 75 for first judge and read along. The reading on the graph gives the score as 64, but since every other score is shown to be a multiple of 5, you could give the answer as 65 also. Either the answer 64 or the answer 65 would get you full marks.

SECTOR

A sector is part of a circle bounded by two radiuses (radii) and the arc between them, as shown.

The *area* of a sector where the radius is r and the angle subtended at the centre of the circle is x, measured in degrees, is given by:

$$\text{area} = \frac{x}{360} \, \pi r^2$$

The *arc length* of the sector is given by:

$$\text{arc length} = \frac{x}{360} \, \pi D$$

where D is the diameter of the circle.

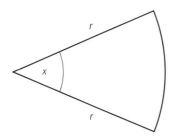

Sector

Exam Question

A keyhole is shown, represented by a circle and a triangle overlapping. The perimeter of the keyhole consists of two straight lines and two arcs of circles, one of radius 7 cm and the other of radius 2 cm. Both circles have centre O.

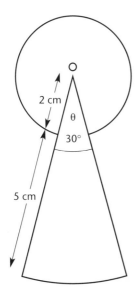

A formula for the length of an arc of a circle is given by:

$$\text{arc length} = \frac{\theta \times \pi \times r}{180}$$

where r is the radius of the circle and $\theta°$ is the angle at the centre of the circle.

(a) Calculate the perimeter of the keyhole.
(b) A keyhole is draughtproof if its perimeter is no more than 3 times the thickness of the door. What is the minimum thickness of door for which this keyhole is draughtproof?

(NEAB; H)

Solution

(a) Bottom arc $= \dfrac{30 \times \pi \times 7}{180} = 3.7$ cm

Top arc $= \dfrac{330 \times \pi \times 2}{180} = 11.5$ cm

So the total perimeter will be 3.7 + 11.5 + 10 = 25.2 cm

(b) 25.2 cm ÷ 3 = 8.4 cm.

SEGMENT

When a circle has a chord drawn in it, as shown, the chord divides the circle into two segments. The larger one is called the *major segment*; the smaller one is called the *minor segment*.

Angles in a segment

⊹ *Angles*

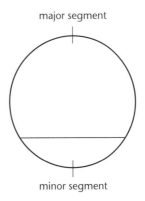

Segment

SEMICIRCLE

A semicircle is exactly half of the circle, as shown.

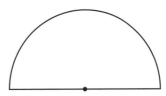

A triangle drawn in a semicircle such that two vertices are on the end of the diameter and the other vertex is somewhere on the arc, is a right-angled triangle, the right angle being opposite to the diameter, which is the hypotenuse.

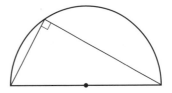

SEMI-INTERQUARTILE RANGE

The semi-interquartile range is exactly half of the interquartile range.

-+- *Interquartile range*

SEPTAGON

A septagon is a seven-sided plane figure, i.e. a **polygon**. It is also called a heptagon. A regular septagon has seven **lines of symmetry**, one through each angle bisector and **rotational symmetry** of order seven.

SEQUENCE

A sequence is a list of numbers that follow some regular, set pattern. For example:

1, 4, 9, 16, 25, 36	n^2
2, 4, 6, 8, 10, 12	$2n$
2, 6, 12, 20, 30	$(n + 1) . (n + 2)$

Notice how the *n*th term has been indicated also. Every sequence that follows a pattern has an *n*th term and examination questions will often ask for this. A *linear sequence* is one when the difference between the two consecutive terms is always the same. In a *quadratic sequence* the difference between consecutive terms increases. Perhaps the best place to test this ability of spotting patterns and generalizing them is within your coursework, and in particular during investigations.

-+- *Generalize, Number patterns*

SIGNIFICANT FIGURES

We use significant figures whenever we estimate or make a guess at a number. A number having a specific significant figure will have that many actual digits, with the rest being zeros to keep place value. For example, look at the following table which illustrates various numbers of significant figures:

One significant figure	5	10	400	0.09	0.0006
Two significant figures	12	450	8,300	0.37	0.029
Three significant figures	214	9,560	2.65	0.0429	0.00176

We often need to **round** off to so many significant figures. When this happens we need simply to look at the first digit that 'has to go':

- If it's less than a 5 we round *down*.

- If it's a 5 or more we round *up*.

> Remember: When you round off to estimate an answer to a problem, you will round off to one significant figure.

So, for example, look at the following table to see how this has been achieved for the numbers chosen:

Number	34.87	159.2	10,982
One significant figure	30	200	10,000
Two significant figures	35	160	11,000
Three significant figures	34.9	159	11,000

This topic is seldom examined on its own; it will come into a question as 'give your answer to two significant figures'. If you don't follow such instructions then you will lose marks. The biggest error on this topic is that candidates do not round off because they fail to read the *accuracy limit* on a question. Or, of course, they fail to recognize a situation where they need to *choose* to round off to so many significant figures

Golden rule: 'if in any doubt, round off to one more significant figure than those given in the question'. This rule only applies if you have a doubt about the intention of the question.

SIMILAR FIGURES

Two shapes are said to be (mathematically) similar if all their corresponding angles are equal and the ratios of the corresponding lengths are also equal.

For example, all the *corresponding angles* in the pair of triangles shown, as you can see, are equal and the ratio of each pair of corresponding sides are equal at 1:3

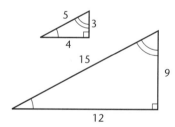

Similar figures

Ratios of similar shapes

For a pair of similar shapes there is always the following relationship between the ratios of lengths, areas and volumes. Namely,

- When the ratio of lengths is $x:y$

- Then the ratio of areas is $x^2:y^2$

- And the ratio of volumes is $x^3:y^3$

This relationship is best learnt; it nearly always crops up on examination papers somewhere.

As an example, in the Ecclesall Badminton league the winning team has a silver cup weighing 6 kg and 30 cm high. Each member gets a silver replica of the cup, each one 10 cm high. The full size cup and the replicas are similar shapes; what is the weight of each replica?

The ratio of the *lengths* is 10:30 which simplifies down to 1:3; hence the ratio of the *volumes* (which is what we need to consider the weight) is $1 \times 1 \times 1$ to $3 \times 3 \times 3$ which is 1:27

Hence the weight of the replica will be 6 kg divided by 27, which gives 0.2222222, which we shall round off to 0.22 kg or 220 g.

Exam Question

The model railway gauge called N-gauge is at a scale of 1:160. The area of a sign was 4,000 cm². Calculate the area of the model sign of the platform in N-gauge.

(NEAB; H)

Solution

$4{,}000 \div (160)^2 = 0.156$ cm²

Exam Questions

1. A badge is made in two sizes.

The area of the small badge is 3 cm².
The large badge is an enlargement of the small badge in the ratio 2:3
Calculate the area of the large badge.

2. Find the height of a tree which casts a shadow of 1.2 metres, when at the same moment in the same place a woman of height 140 cm casts a shadow of 60 cm.

Solutions

1. The length ratio is 2:3
    The area ratio is $2^2:3^2 = 4 : 9$
    The area of the larger badge = $3 \times \frac{9}{4} = 6.75$ cm²
2. The question can be illustrated by two similar triangles as shown,

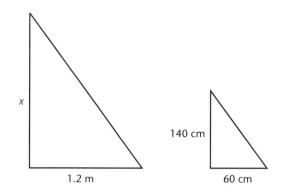

$\dfrac{x}{1.2} = \dfrac{140}{60} \rightarrow x = \dfrac{1.2 \times 140}{60} = 2.8$ metres

SIMPLE INTEREST

Simple interest (SI) is the amount of money given as a result of leaving a sum of money with a bank, etc., for a particular time. It is calculated on the basis of having a *principal amount*, P, in the bank for a number of years T, with a rate of interest R. There is then a simple formula to work out the amount of simple interest the money will earn:

$$\text{SI} = \frac{P \times R \times T}{100}$$

For example, Michael put £5 in a society that paid him 9% simple interest. Calculate how much interest he would earn on this amount in 10 years.

Where the principal P is £5, the time T is 10 years and the rate R is 9%, then using the formula $(\text{SI} = {}^{PRT}\!/_{100})$ gives us

$$\text{SI} = \frac{5 \times 9 \times 10}{100} = £4.50$$

✦ *Compound interest*

SIMPLIFICATION

This is the process of making an algebraic expression simpler. It consists of either **factorizing** or multiplying out and collecting 'like' terms. In other words, doing anything that makes the expression simpler. For example:

● $3x – 9y$ would simplify to $3(x – 3y)$

● $x^2 + 6x + 5$ would simplify to $(x + 5)(x + 1)$
These two have been factorized.

● $5(x + 2y) + 2(4x – 3y) = 5x + 10y + 8x – 6y = 13x + 4y$
This has been *expanded* and then *simplified*.

Exam Question

Simplify $3(2x – 1) –2(3x – 4)$

(NEAB; I)

Solution

$6x – 3 – 6x + 8 = 5$

SIMULTANEOUS EQUATIONS

Simultaneous equations are a pair (at least) of equations that need solving at the same time so that the solution satisfies both of them.

The technique is simply to eliminate one variable and to solve for the single variable in the resulting simplified equation. Then to substitute that value back into one of the given equations in order to solve for the other variable. Here are two examples:

1. Solve $3x + y = 11$ . . . . . (i)
    $\qquad\quad 4x – y = 3$ . . . . . . (ii)

● By adding the two equations, we eliminate y:
$7x = 14$

● Hence $x = 2$

● Substitute this value into equation (i)
to give $6 + y = 11$

● Hence $y = 5$

● So the solution is $x = 2$, $y = 5$

This should be checked in equation (ii) as $8 - 5 = 3$,
which is correct.

2. Solve $5x + 4y = 21$ . . . . . (i)
$\qquad 3x + 2y = 12$ . . . . . (ii)

● We need to multiply equation (ii) by 2
$\qquad 6x + 4y = 24$ . . . . . (iii)

● Subtract equation (i) from equation (iii) to
eliminate y

● Hence $x = 3$

● Substitute into equation (i)
to give $15 + 4y = 21$
$\qquad\qquad 4y = 6$

● Hence $\qquad y = 1.5$

Check the solution in equation (ii) as $9 + 3 = 12$,
which is correct. Hence our solution is $x = 3$ and
$y = 1.5$

⊹ *Equations*

Exam Question

The first three hexagonal numbers 1, 7 and 19 are
shown in the dot patterns.

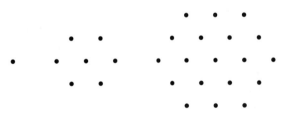

(a) Find the fourth hexagonal number.
(b) The nth hexagonal number is given by an expression
of the form $an^2 + bn + 1$, where a and b are
numerical constants. Using the information above,
write down two simultaneous equations in a and b
and solve them to find a and b.
(c) Verify that the 7th, 9th, 10th and 16th hexagonal
numbers all contain the same three digits.

(NEAB; H)

Solution

(a) 37
(b) When $n = 1$, $an^2 + bn + 1 = 1$, hence $a + b = 0$
When $n = 2$, $an^2 + bn + 1 = 7$, hence $4a + 2b = 6$
i.e. $\quad a + b = 0$ . . (i)
$\qquad 2a + b = 3$ . . (ii)
subtract (i) from (ii) to give $a = 3$
substitute in (i) to give $b = -3$

(c) Hence the nth hexagonal number is $3n^2 - 3n + 1$, so:
when $n = 7$, $3n^2 - 3n + 1 = 127$
when $n = 9$, $3n^2 - 3n + 1 = 217$
when $n = 10$, $3n^2 - 3n + 1 = 271$
when $n = 16$, $3n^2 - 3n + 1 = 721$
each one uses the digits 1, 2 and 7.

Exam Question
Solve the following simultaneous equations:
$4x - 3y = 18$
$5x + 2y = 11$

Solution
the aim is to get the ys the same, so that we can add two
equations together to eliminate the ys
Multiply the top equation by 2, and the bottom
equation by 3:

$\quad 8x - 6y = 36$
$\underline{15x + 6y = 33}$ $\quad$ add
$\overline{23x \qquad = 69}$
$\qquad x = 69 \div 23 = 3$
$\qquad x = 3$

substitute $x = 3$ into the bottom equation:
$15 + 2y = 11$
$\quad 2y = 11 - 15 = -4$
$\quad y = -4 \div 2 = -2$

the solution is $x = 3$ and $y = -2$

CHECKPOINT

Solve:
$3x + 2y = 29$
$5x - 2y = 11$

SINE

Sine is a trigonometrical ratio that every angle has. In
a *right-angled triangle*, the sine is defined for an angle
by the side opposite divided by the hypotenuse:

$$\text{sine} = \frac{\text{side opposite}}{\text{hypotenuse}}$$

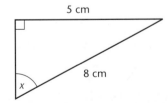

For example from the lengths seen in the triangle,
the sine of angle x (called sin x) is usually found by
dividing 5 cm (side opposite) by 8 cm (hypotenuse).
This gives 0.625. So sin $x = 0.625$

We can use this fact to calculate the size of angle
x. With 0.625 in the calculator, press $\boxed{\text{INV}}$ $\boxed{\text{sin}}$ (or
$\boxed{\text{sin}^{-1}}$) and the angle should appear on the display.

In a second example we can find the length of a
side. So, from the triangle shown we can state that
the sine of angle 35 is y divided by 6 cm.

Hence $y/6 = \sin 35$, and $y = 6 \sin 35$

Calculate this in the calculator by putting in 35, pressing $\boxed{\sin}$, then multiplying by 6 to give us 3.4414586, which we would round off to 3.4 cm.

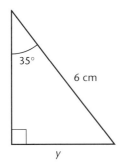

SINE CURVE

The graph shown is of $y = \sin x$ and shows the sine curve. It is symmetrical about $x = 90°$ and $x = 270°$, hence you will see that what is drawn is only part of the whole curve. The sine curve continues in this form along both the positive and the negative x axis.

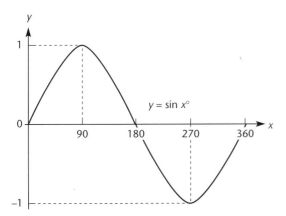

Sine curve

This symmetrical pattern should help you to see that if you are given an angle, A, greater than 90°, then its sine will be the same as sin (180 – A).

Your calculator will automatically give you the right sine for the angle you put into the calculator. But if, for example, you had to find what angle has a sine of 0.325, then the calculator will only tell you 19° (rounded off). There is of course another angle (180 – 19) which is 161°. You may realize that in fact there are lots more angles that have the sine of 0.325, which can be found by continuing the sine curve beyond 360°; but this is A level work! (This is a Higher Level only topic.)

SINE RULE

The sine rule works in any triangle and is illustrated on the triangle shown:

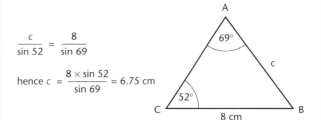

$$\frac{a}{\sin A} = \frac{b}{\sin B} = \frac{c}{\sin C}$$

$$\frac{\sin A}{a} = \frac{\sin B}{b} = \frac{\sin C}{c}$$

Sine rule

The sine rule is used either way up, as necessary, when you are given 3 pieces of information about two angles and their opposite sides. Use the rule in such a way that the 'thing' you're looking for appears first in your formula. For example, in the figure below, to find the length of side c, use the rule as:

$$\frac{c}{\sin 52} = \frac{8}{\sin 69}$$

hence $c = \dfrac{8 \times \sin 52}{\sin 69} = 6.75$ cm

(This is a Higher Level only topic.)

CHECKPOINT

(a) What is the sine of 40°
(b) What angle has a sine of 0.456

SKETCH GRAPHS

⇌ *Graphs*

SOLID SHAPES

Solid shapes are three-dimensional figures, and you should be familiar with the following names and facts:

● A *cube* has all its sides the same length; each face is a square;
volume = length^3

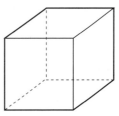

Cube

● A *cuboid* has each opposite edge the same length; each face is a rectangle;
volume = length × breadth × height.

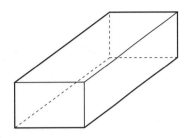

Cuboid

● A *sphere*: the distance from the centre of the sphere to its outer edge is constant and is called its *radius* (r)
volume $= \frac{4}{3} \times \pi \times r^3$
surface area $= 4 \times \pi \times r^2$

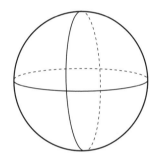

Sphere

● A *cylinder* is a prism whose regular cross section is a circle:
volume = π × radius² × height
curved surface area = 2 × π × radius × height
total surface area = 2 × π × radius × height *plus*
2 × π × radius²

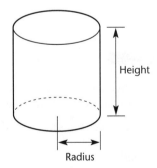

Cylinder

● A *pyramid*: the base can be any shape; from each point on the perimeter of the base there is a straight line that goes up to the same point at the top (the *vertex*);
volume $= \frac{1}{3}$ × base area × height.

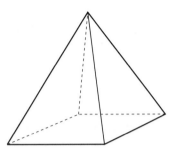

Pyramid

● A *cone* is a pyramid with a circular base; when a *cone* of height *h* has a base radius *r* and a slant height of *l*
volume $= \frac{1}{3} \times \pi \times r^2 \times h$
curved surface area (CSA) = πrl

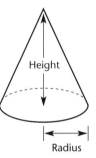

Cone

Words connected with solids are *edge*, *face* and *vertex* (plural *vertices*):

● An edge is a line where two faces meet.

● A face is the flat surface of a solid shape.

● A vertex is a point where two or more edges meet.

Exam Question
Assume that the Earth is a sphere having a diameter of 12,576 km. It is known that about $\frac{2}{3}$ of the Earth's surface is covered by water.
(a) Write the diameter of the Earth
  (i) correct to 3 significant figures,
  (ii) in standard form, correct to 3 significant figures.
(b) Calculate the approximate area (in km²) of the Earth's surface which is covered by water.

(NEAB; H)

Solution
(a) (i) 12,600 km
  (ii) 1.26×10^4
(b) Surface area of a sphere = $4\pi r^2$
  $= 4 \times \pi \times 6{,}288^2 = 469{,}861{,}024$
  $\frac{2}{3}$ of this $= 331{,}000{,}000$ km²

SOLUTION SETS

A solution set is the set of points that form the solution to some problem involving inequalities. For example, in the figure shown, a solution set could be all the points in the region unshaded. It is usual to make solution sets the *unshaded* region as it is then easier to see what points there are in that set. (This is a Higher Level only topic.)

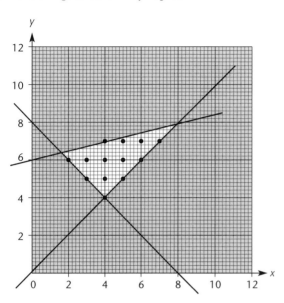

> *Remember: In situations like these, it is only the integer co-ordinates that we are interested in, and our solutions are always in one of the corners.*

Exam Question

An education authority plans to build a school in a new housing estate. There are two types of teaching area, classrooms which each occupy 100 m² and practical rooms which each occupy 130 m². The maximum area allocated in total for these two types of rooms is 3,900 m².

(a) If x is the number of classrooms and y the number of practical rooms show that $10x + 13y \leqslant 390$.
(b) A classroom accommodates 35 pupils and a practical room 20 pupils. At least 700 pupils are to be accommodated. Show that $7x + 4y \geqslant 140$.
(c) The number of classrooms must not exceed the number of practical rooms by more than 5. Illustrate this condition by an inequality.
(d) The number of classrooms must be at least 13. Illustrate this condition by an inequality.
(e) Using a scale of 2 cm to represent 5 units on each axis, illustrate these four inequalities by a suitable diagram on graph paper.
(f) From the solution set find
   (i) the minimum and maximum number of classrooms which could be built
   (ii) the solution (x, y) which gives the maximum number of teaching areas.
(g) What is the maximum number of pupils that could be accommodated in the school under the above four conditions?

(NISEAC; H)

Solution

(a) $100x + 130y \leqslant 3,900$
   divide throughout by 10 to give $10x + 13y \leqslant 390$
(b) $35x + 20y \geqslant 700$
   divide throughout by 5 to give $7x + 4y \geqslant 140$
(c) $x - y \leqslant 5$
(d) $x \geqslant 13$
(e) The unshaded region in the figure shown is the solution set.

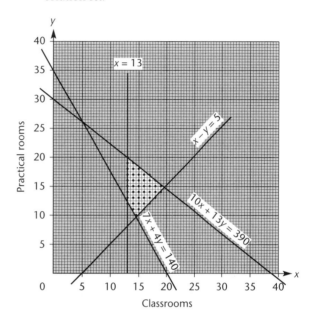

(f) (i) minimum number = (14, 11) or (15, 10) = 25
       maximum number = (19, 15) = 34
   (ii) the solution (19, 15)
(g) Maximum pupils is still at the point (19, 15), which is $(35 \times 19) + (20 \times 15) = 965$

SOLVE

To solve a *problem* is to find the answer to it. To solve an *equation* is to find the number that satisfies the equation. For example, solve $4x + 3 = 23$.

The only value of x that satisfies this equation, and therefore makes the statement correct, is $x = 5$.

Exam Question

(a) Basil, a window cleaner, put his 5-metre long ladder against a vertical wall to make an angle of 75° with the ground, as shown. How far up the wall did the ladder reach?
(b) If he placed the foot of the ladder 90 cm away from the wall, how far up the wall would his ladder reach?

(NEAB; I)

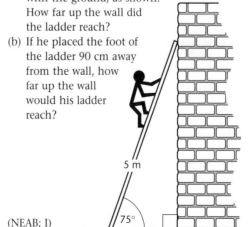

Solution

(a) Recognize the trigonometry sine situation, to give:

$$\frac{\text{opposite}}{\text{hypotenuse}} =$$

$$\frac{\text{opposite (height)}}{5} = \sin 75°$$

Hence height = 5 sin 75° = 4.83 or 4.8 m.

(b) Recognize the Pythagoras situation, to give:

height^2 = 5^2 – (0.9)^2

= 24.19

height = $\sqrt{(24.19)}$ = 4.92 or 4.9 m

SPEED

Speed is the rate of change of distance. It can be found by the **gradient** of a distance/time graph.

Average speed

Average speed is found by the total distance travelled divided by the total travelling time. The *units* of speed can vary with the data used to calculate it.

For example James cycled 28 miles in 2 hours, or $\frac{28}{2}$ = 14 miles per hour. John ran 10,000 metres in 28 minutes, or $\frac{10,000}{28}$ = 357 metres per minute.

CHECKPOINT

How can

'Diana of Star Trek'

help you to remember the speed rules?

⟿ *Gradient, Travel graphs*

SPHERE

A sphere is a solid shape. Every point on its outer surface is the same distance from the centre of the sphere. A sphere is a ball-shape, and the shape of the world is used as a sphere for the sake of calculations.

● The volume of a sphere is equal to $\frac{4}{3} \times \pi \times$ radius^3

● The surface area of a sphere is equal to $4 \times \pi \times$ radius^2

⟿ *Solid shapes, Sphere*

SQUARE

A square has all its four sides equal and all its angles are right angles. A square has **rotational symmetry** of order 4, because if you turn it round its centre, there are four different positions it can take that all look the same, as shown.

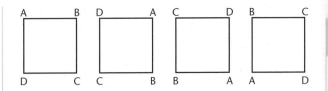

Square numbers

A square *number* is one that has a **factor** which can multiply by itself to give this square number. For example, 16 has the factor 4 and we know that $4 \times 4 = 16$. The first few square numbers are 1, 4, 9, 16, 25, 36, 49, 64 and 81.

Square roots

The square *root* of a number is that number that multiplies by itself to give you that number. For example, the square root of 9 is 3, since $3 \times 3 = 9$.

Of course if a number has an **integer** square root, then this number is a square number.

You find square roots on your calculator by pressing the button with $\boxed{\sqrt{}}$ on it. Every number has two square roots, one positive the other negative. For example, the square roots of 25 are 5 and –5.

STANDARD FORM

Standard form is a convenient way of writing very large or very small numbers. It is always expressed in the terms of:

$$a \times 10^N$$

Where a is a number between 1 and 10, and N is an integer.

For example:

400	would be written as	4.0×10^2
35,687	would be written as	3.5687×10^4
132.98	would be written as	1.3298×10^2

> *Remember: Most calculators do not put the × 10 in, but leave you to recognize that 3.142 5 means 3.142×10^5.*

Note how the index on the 10 tells you how many places to move the decimal point. If the number is less than 0 to start with then the index will be negative. For example:

0.000000037	would be written as	3.7×10^{-8}
0.0020005	would be written as	2.0005×10^{-3}

Exam Question

A pack of 52 playing cards is 1.5 cm thick. Write down, in standard form, the thickness, in cm, of one playing card.

(NEAB; I)

Solution

$1.5 \div 52 = 0.0288$
$\qquad = 2.88 \times 10^{-2}$

Exam Question

The mass of one atom of oxygen is given as
2.66×10^{-23} grams
The mass of one atom of hydrogen is given as
1.67×10^{-24} grams
(a) Find the difference in mass between one atom of
oxygen and one atom of hydrogen.
(b) A molecule of water contains two atoms of hydrogen
and one atom of oxygen.
(i) Calculate the mass of one molecule of water.
(ii) Calculate the number of molecules of water in
1,000 grams of water.

Solution

(a) Subtract the numbers on your calculator in standard
form to give you: 2.493×10^{-23}
(b) (i) $2 \times 1.67 \times 10^{-24} + 2.66 \times 10^{-23} = 2.994 \times 10^{-23}$ g
(ii) $1,000$ grams $\div 2.994 \times 10^{-23} = 3.34 \times 10^{25}$

CHECKPOINT

Write as standard form:

(a) Five million.
(b) One millionth.

-+- *Index*

STATISTICS

Statistics are pieces of information. Statistical *methods*
help us express information in a way that makes the
information clear. This may involve using charts and
diagrams, and making simple calculations.
Questions are always asked on statistics in your
examinations and, if you read the question carefully,
then they should be relatively easy questions to
answer.

-+- *Bar charts, pictograms, pie charts, histograms,
averages, frequency*

SUBSTITUTION

Substitution is where you put a particular value in
place of a variable in an expression or a formula.
For example, if I substitute $x = 3$ into the equation
$y = 5x + 2$, then the value of y will become
$y = 5 \times 3 + 2 = 17$.

Exam Question

Calculate the exact value of $x^2 - 4x - 1$
(a) when $x = -1$
(b) when $x = 2.56$.

Solution

(a) $1 - -4 - 1 = 1 + 4 - 1 = 4$
(b) $6.5536 - 10.24 - 1 = -4.6864$

Exam Question

Given that $m = \frac{1}{2}$, $p = \frac{3}{4}$ and $t = -5$
calculate
(a) $mp + t$
(b) $\dfrac{(m + p)}{t}$

Solution

(a) $\frac{1}{2} \times \frac{3}{4} - 5 = \frac{3}{8} - 5 = -4\frac{5}{8}$ or -4.625
(b) $\dfrac{(\frac{1}{2} + \frac{3}{4})}{-5} = \dfrac{1\frac{1}{4}}{-5} = -0.25$

SUBTRACTING/SUBTRACTION

-+- *Directed numbers*

SURVEYS

A survey is an organized way of asking a lot of
people a few well-constructed questions, or making a
lot of observations in an experiment in order to
reach a conclusion about something.
We use surveys to test out people's opinions or to
test out a hypothesis that has been suggested.

SYMMETRY

Symmetry is found in two- and three-dimensional
shapes.

Two-dimensional symmetry

There are two particular types of symmetry:

Line

If you can fold a shape over so that one half fits
exactly on top of the other half, then the line over
which you have folded is called a **line of symmetry**.
The examples shown illustrate this. The dashed lines
are lines of symmetry.

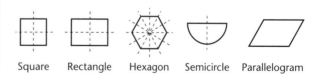

Square   Rectangle   Hexagon   Semicircle   Parallelogram

Exam Question
(a) Draw in all the lines of symmetry of the shapes
below.

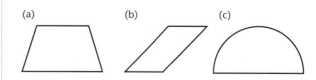

(b) State the order of rotational symmetry of the figure
below.

(a)   (b)   (c)

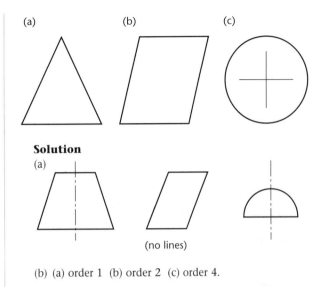

Solution

(a)

(no lines)

(b) (a) order 1   (b) order 2   (c) order 4.

> *Remember: A regular **N**-sided polygon has **N** lines of symmetry and rotational symmetry of order **N**.*

Rotational symmetry

This is sometimes called *point symmetry*. A shape has rotational symmetry according to how many different positions it can be turned round to so as to look exactly the same.

For example, a square has rotational symmetry of order 4, since if you turn it round its centre there are four different positions that it can take that all look the same, as shown.

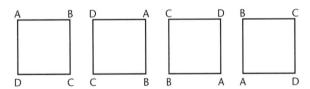

The orders of rotational symmetry of a variety of shapes have been given. Any shape that has what we call 'no symmetry', such as the letter Q, has rotational symmetry of order 1, since there is only one position in which it looks the same.

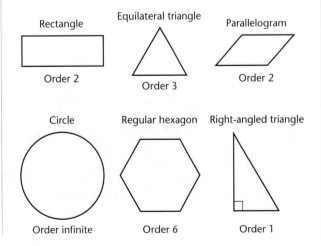

Rectangle — Order 2

Equilateral triangle — Order 3

Parallelogram — Order 2

Circle — Order infinite

Regular hexagon — Order 6

Right-angled triangle — Order 1

Exam Question

(a) Four square tiles are shown with a pattern drawn on the top left-hand tile. Draw the patterns needed on the other three tiles so that the completed picture is symmetrical about the line AB and about the line CD.

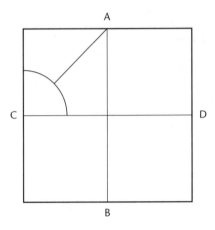

AB and CD intersect at the point 0, which is not labelled in the diagram.

Write down a statement that describes the rotational symmetry of the finished pattern about 0.

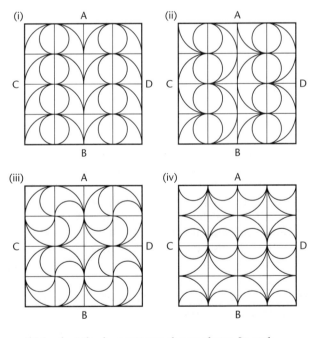

(b) Look at the four patterns shown above. In each pattern, 0 is the point of intersection of AB and CD.

Pattern IV has a tick in the box for rotational symmetry of 180° about 0, because if the pattern is rotated about 0 through 180° then the pattern would look unchanged.

Pattern	Symmetrical about AB	Symmetrical about CD	Rotational symmetry of 180° about 0
I			
II			
III			
IV			✓

For each pattern in turn, place a tick (✓) in the box if the pattern has the property. A pattern may have more than one of the symmetries given in the table.

(WJEC; I)

Solution

(a)

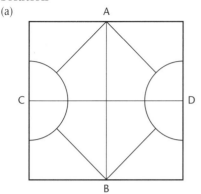

Rotational symmetry of order 2.

(b)

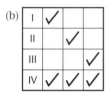

I	✓		
II		✓	
III			✓
IV	✓	✓	✓

Three-dimensional symmetry

Planes of symmetry

A shape has a plane of symmetry if you can slice the shape into two matching pieces, one the exact mirror image of the other. To find these planes of symmetry you need to be able to visualize the shape being cut and to see in your mind whether the pieces are matching mirror images or not.

For example, a cuboid has three planes of symmetry, as shown by the accompanying diagrams.

Find how many planes of symmetry a cuboid has

Consider the cuboid shown above. We can cut it into two exact halves in the following three ways. Hence the shape has three planes of symmetry.

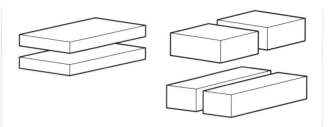

Axes of symmetry

An ***axis of symmetry*** is a line through which the shape may rotate and yet still occupy the same space.

For example, in the square-based pyramid shown, there is an *axis of symmetry* along the line through the vertex and the centre of the base. Around this axis the shape has ***rotational symmetry*** of order four, since it can occupy four different positions within the same space.

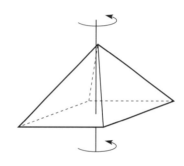

A cuboid has three different *axes of symmetry*.

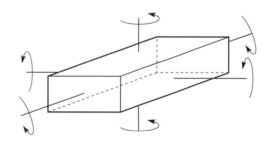

CHECKPOINT

Describe the symmetries of:

(a) A regular nonagon.
(b) A parallelogram.

TABLES

Tables are 'containers' of information which are set out in an orderly way and are largely numeric. There are a number of tables that you ought to be confident in using.

Types of tables

Timetables

The table shows an example of a timetable. You should be able to work out times of buses from one place to another as well as be able to plan out a journey using timetables like these.

SHEFFIELD CITY SERVICE							ONE MAN Service
CITY · GREYSTONES · NORTON							**40**

Monday to Friday only

		⊗			⊗	□		
ARUNDEL GATE	....	....	0820	1230	1530	1530	1610	1710
Hunters Bar	....	0805	0835	1245	1545	1545	1625	1725
Ecclesall, Knowle Lane		0816	0846	♥	1556	♥	1636	1736
Millhouses, Springfield Road		0822	0852	....	1602	....	....	....
Abbey Lane, Bocking Lane		0827	....	....	1607	....	....	....
Meadowhead, Norton Hotel		0834	....	....	1614	....	....	....
NORTON, Cloonmore Drive		0837	....	....	1617	....	....	....

	⊗	□		⊗	□	
NORTON, Cloonmore Drive	0755	0840	....	....	....	1521	....
Meadowhead, Norton Hotel	0758	0843	....	....	....	1524	....
Abbey Lane, Bocking Lane	0805	0850	....	....	....	1531	....
Millhouses, Springfield Road	0810	0855	0855	....	....	1536	....
Ecclesall, Knowle Lane	0816	0901	0901	●	●	1542	●
Hunters Bar	0826	0911	0911	0941	1251	1557	1557
ARUNDEL GATE	0842	0927	0927	0957	1307	1613	1613

CODE

⊗ – Runs Schooldays only.   □ – Not Schooldays.

♥ – Runs to Rustlings Road Junction.

● – Starts from Rustlings Road Junction 1 minute before time shown for Hunters Bar

Timetable

Tidetables

The tidetable shows the approximate times of the high tides for the first ten days in February 1999. You will read that the high tide on February 8th was at 0829, which is twenty nine minutes past eight in the morning, and 2046, which is fourteen minutes to nine in the evening.

	Tidetable **February 1999**					
	Morning			*Afternoon*		
Date	Time	Height		Time	Height	Moon
		Mtrs	Ft ins		Mtrs	Ft ins	
1	0449	3.20	10.5	1711	3.20	10.5	
2	0526	3.60	11.8	1746	3.51	11.5	F.M.
3	0600	3.75	12.3	1818	3.60	11.8	
4	0631	3.87	12.7	1848	3.60	11.8	
5	0702	3.87	12.7	1917	3.60	11.8	
6	0730	3.87	12.7	1947	3.60	11.8	
S 7	0759	3.75	12.3	2015	3.38	11.1	
8	0829	3.51	11.5	2046	3.08	10.1	
9	0900	3.20	10.5	2119	2.87	9.4	
10	0936	2.87	9.4	2200	2.47	8.1	Last Qtr

Insurance tables

You can see from the insurance table given that costs vary for different ages and for the amount of insurance required.

Insurance table				
Monthly insurance premiums				
Age (next)	£1000	£5000	£10,000	£50,000
20	1.65	7.80	14.50	55.10
25	1.90	8.15	16.20	63.80
30	2.40	9.00	17.65	68.10
35	3.45	10.05	19.95	77.90
40	6.55	18.95	37.40	165.50
45	15.80			

For female substract 5 years from current age

Cost table

The table shows you the different charges for first class and second class post at a particular date.

Cost table					
Postal information inland					
Weight (g) not exceeding	First class	Second class	Weight (g) not exceeding	First class	Second class
	p	p	350(12.3oz)	61	46
60 (2.1oz)	19	14	400 (14.1oz)	69	52
100 (3.5oz)	24	18	450 (15.9oz)	78	59
150 (5.3oz)	31	22	500 (1.1lb)	87	66
200 (7.1oz)	38	28	750 (1.7lb)	128	98
250 (8.8oz)	45	34	1,000 (2.2lb)	170	max
300 (10.6oz)	53	40	Each extra 250g (18.8oz)	42	–

Registration: Minimum fee, £1; compensation up to £500.

Recorded delivery: Letters and Packets: fee, 20p in addition to postage. Compensation up to £18.

Exam Question

(a) Repayment details are shown for various amounts of a loan. Some of the figures in the table have been obscured by a coffee stain.

REPAYMENT PEROID	48 MONTHS	60 MONTHS	72 MONTHS
LOAN AMOUNT	MONTHLY REPAYMENTS (total amount payable in brackets)		
£3,000	£87.19 (£4,185.12)	£75.20	
£4,000	(£5,580.00)		
£5,000	£145.31 (£6,974.88)	£12 (£7,520.40)	
£7,500	£217.97 (£10,462.56)	£188.01 (£11,280.60)	(£12,

Use the table to answer the questions below.

(i) If you take a loan of £3,000 and pay it back over 60 months, calculate the total amount you pay back.

(ii) How much would you pay back per month for a loan of £4,000 over 48 months?

(iii) Work out the monthly repayment for a loan of £3,800 over 4 years.

(b) The timetable at the bottom of this page shows the times of the 327 bus on Sundays.

(i) What is the latest time you can catch a bus from Luton to Rickmansworth?

(ii) How many minutes does the bus take to travel from St Albans Bus Garage to Watford Junction?

(iii) How many journeys are made by a 327 bus on Sundays from Luton to Rickmansworth?

Solution

(a) (i) £75.20 × 60 = £4,512

(ii) £5,580 ÷ 48 = £116.25

(iii) £1,000 will cost £87.19 ÷ 3 hence £3,800 will be £87.19 ÷ 3 × 3.8 = £110.44

(b) (i) 1,850 or ten to seven.

(ii) From 23 to 52 or from 17 to 46 minutes past the hour. This gives a time of 29 minutes.

(iii) There are 11.

TALLY CHART

A tally chart is a chart that helps us to keep count of different events during some experiment or trial.

For example, if you were doing a count of the favourite flavour crisp at your school or college you could use a tabular chart as shown. Each time you ask someone their favourite flavour, you put a mark in the correct row. When you wish to put down the fifth mark you put a diagonal line across the others, like a bar on a gate as shown. This way you can more easily count them all up at the end. If someone wants a flavour that you haven't got, you put that mark in the row headed 'others'.

From the tally chart you would then construct a *frequency* table of some sort.

Tally		
Flavour	*Tally*	*Total*
Plain	⁙⁙⁙ ‖	17
Salt 'n vinegar	⁙⁙⁙⁙⁙⁙ ‖‖	34
Cheese & onion	⁙⁙ ‖	11
Others	⁙⁙ ‖‖	13

Remember: If you are asked to tally, you should demonstrate the 'gateing' to show you do know it.

Sundays and Public Holidays (Bus 327)

Luton *Bus station*				0850		50	1750	1850						
Lantern Fields *Slip End Turn*				0859		59	1759	1859						
Kingbourne *Green Harrow*				0904		04	1804	1904						
Harpenden *George*				0910	Then	10	1810	1910						
Sandingabury Lane				0920	at	20	1820	1920						
St Albans *Bus Garage* (A)				0923	these	23	1823	1917	1923	2023	2123	2217	2317	
St Albans *St Peters Street*				0924	minutes	24	UNTIL 1824	1918	1924	2024	2124	2218	2318	
Chiswell Green *Three Hammers*				0933	past	33	1833	1927	1933	2033	2133	2227	2327	
Garston Watford *Bus Garage*	0720	0758	0841	0941	each	41	1841	1935	1941	2041	2141	2235	2335	
Watford Junction	0731	0809	0852	0952	hour	52	1852		1952	2052	2152	2246		
Watford *Town Centre*	0734	0812	0855	0955		55	1855		1955	2055	2155	2249		
Croxley Green Station			0819	0902	1002		02	1902		2002	2102	2202	2256	
Croxley Green *Manor Way*			0823	0906	1006		06	1906		2006	2106	2206	2300	
Rickmansworth *Station*				0915	1015		15	1915		2015	2115	2215		

TANGENT

There are two uses of the word tangent in mathematics.

Tangent in trigonometry

Tan, which is short for tangent, is a *trigonometrical ratio* that every angle has. The tan ratio is defined for an angle in a right-angled triangle, by the side opposite divided by the side adjacent

$$\tan = \frac{\text{side opposite}}{\text{side adjacent}}$$

For example, from the lengths shown in the triangle the tan of angle x (tan x) is found by dividing 8 cm (side opposite) by 5 cm (side adjacent). This gives 1.6, so tan x = 1.6

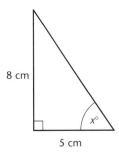

We can use this fact to calculate the size of angle x. With 1.6 in the calculator, press ⃞INV⃞ ⃞tan⃞ (or ⃞tan⁻¹⃞) and the angle should appear on the display as 58° (rounded off).

In the triangle shown below we can state that the tan of angle 29° is y divided by 6 cm.

Hence $y/6$ = tan 29°, so y = 6 × tan 29°

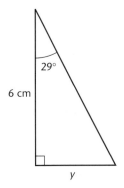

Work this out in the calculator by putting in 29, pressing ⃞tan⃞ and then multiplying by 6 to get 3.325843, which would round off to 3.3 cm.

Tan curve

(Higher Level only.) The graph shows y = tan x, the tan curve. If you are given an angle, A, greater than 90°, then its tan will be the same as tan (A – 180°).

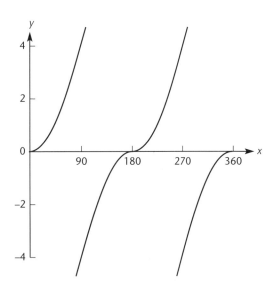

Your calculator will automatically give you the right tan for an angle you put into the calculator. But if, for example, you were to find what angle had a tan of 0.8, then the calculator would tell you 39° (rounded off). There is, however, another angle, 180° + 39° which is 219°.

Tangent to a circle or curve

A tangent to a circle, or a curve, is a line that will touch the circle or curve at only one point.

If drawn to a circle, the tangent is perpendicular to a radius as shown.

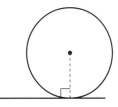

Tangent

There are two ways to draw a tangent to a circle at a particular point. One way is to put your ruler on that point and simply to draw the line that only touches the circle there. This is in fact the only way when it comes to drawing a tangent on a curve (as when finding the ***gradient*** of a curve). The other way is to ***construct*** a right angle at that point on the radius and hence draw in the tangent.

CHECKPOINT

(a) Write down the tangent of 80°
(b) What angle has a tangent of 0.5?
(c) What angle has a tangent of 1.5?

TAXES

Tax is the amount of money that a government tells its people to pay in order to raise sufficient funds for that government to run the country.

Tax systems

The tax system is generally complicated, but you are only expected to be familiar with two major types of tax, VAT and income tax.

VAT

VAT, or value added tax, is the tax put onto the price of goods sold in shops, restaurants, etc., then paid to the government. The tax is usually a percentage and can vary from year to year. The tax also depends on the type of goods being sold, with some goods (such as children's clothes) having a zero rate of VAT, and others the usual 17.5% rate.

Exam Question

A fish and chip shop tells its customers that if they eat their food in the shop then they have to pay VAT at 17.5%; if they eat it outside the shop then they pay no VAT. If it costs £2.10 for fish and chips to eat outside, what will it cost to eat them inside?

Solution

The inside price will be 117.5% of £2.10 which is 210 × $\frac{117.5}{100}$ which is 246.75; this rounds off to £2.46 (note the practice in tax to **truncate** when rounding the tax to be added or paid).

Income tax

Income tax is the type of tax that almost everyone who receives money for working or from investments has to pay to the government. Here again, the amount can change every time the government decides to change it (usually at Budget time). To calculate how much tax you should pay you first need to know the *rate of tax* (a percentage) and your *personal allowances*.

Personal allowances are the amounts of money you may earn before you start to pay tax. It is different for married men, single men and for women in different situations, and can be increased for quite a variety of reasons. Once your personal allowance has been calculated it is divided by ten, truncating the decimal fraction, to give you the number as your *tax code*. For example, a personal allowance of £4,195 will have a tax code of 419.

You only pay tax on your *taxable income*, which is found by subtracting your personal allowance from your total annual income. If your personal allowances are higher than your income, then you pay no income tax.

The rate of tax is expressed either as a percentage, for example 25%, which means that you pay 25% of your taxable income as income tax, or it may be expressed at a certain rate in the £. For example, if it were 24p in the £, you would pay 24p for every £1 of your taxable income (which is equivalent to 24%).

Exam Question

If the rate of tax is 25%, find the income tax paid by Mr Kaye who earns £11,500 per annum and has a tax code of 346.

Solution

Mr Kaye's personal allowance is 346 × 10 = £3,460
hence his taxable income = £11,500 – £3,460 = £8,040
So the tax paid is $\frac{25}{100}$ × £8,040 = £2,010

TERMINATING

✦ *Decimal*

TESSELLATIONS

A *regular* tessellation is a regular pattern with *one shape* that could cover a large area without leaving any gaps (except at the very edge). Some examples of regular tessellations are shown.

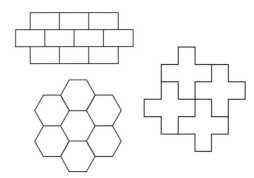

Regular tessellations

Each tessellation is made from one plane shape and could continue its pattern to fill a large area without leaving any space in between. It is true to say that every triangle and every quadrilateral will tessellate.

> Remember: Every triangle, and every quadrilateral will tessellate.

Semi-regular tessellation

A semi-regular tessellation is one which uses more than one shape to create the regular pattern, again leaving no gaps, as shown.

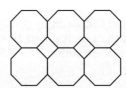

Semi-regular tessellation

Exam Question

Draw a tessellation of the given shape on the grid shown. The shape should be repeated at least eight times.

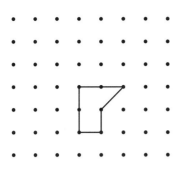

Solution

You should have shown at least 8 shapes fitting to a regular pattern as shown. (There are only two possible patterns.)

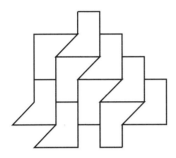

TRANSFORMATIONS

A transformation is a change; within mathematics it often refers to how *plane shapes* change their position and/or shape. The transformations usually covered in a GCSE syllabus will result from:

- Enlargements
- Reflections
- Rotations
- Translations

Examples of plane transformations are shown. However, more detailed explanation will be found under their own reference headings within this guide.

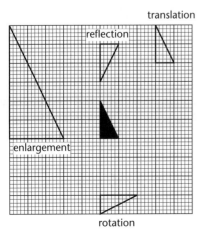

Transformations

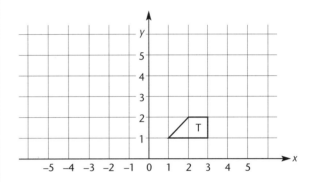

Remember: When you are asked to fully describe a transformation you should give as much information as possible, e.g. lines of reflection, centre of rotations or enlargements, angles with disection.

Exam Question

(a) Trapezium T in the figure is reflected in the line $y = 3$ to give trapezium T_1.
 Trapezium T_1 is then rotated 90° anticlockwise about (0,0) to give trapezium T_2.
 Trapezium T_2 is then translated $\begin{pmatrix} 6 \\ 0 \end{pmatrix}$ to give trapezium T_3.

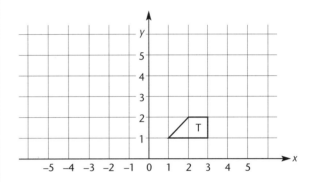

 (i) Show the positions of T_1, T_2 and T_3 on the diagram.
 (ii) Describe the single transformation that would take T to T_3.

(NEAB; I)

(b) Look at the two As shown on the grid. Describe fully two different single transformations which will map the right-hand A onto the left-hand A.

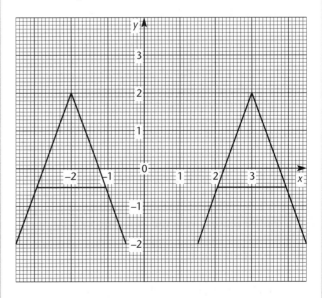

✥ *Enlargements, Reflections, Rotations, Translations*

Solution

(a) (i)

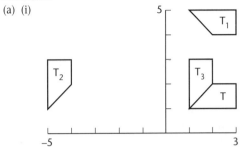

(ii) A reflection in the line $y = x$

(b) (i) A reflection in the line $x = \frac{1}{2}$

(ii) A translation with the vector $\begin{pmatrix} -5 \\ 0 \end{pmatrix}$

(The most common error here would be to misread the question and give the translation as left to right instead of right to left.)

TRANSLATIONS

A translation is a movement along the plane without any rotating, reflecting or enlarging. It is described by a movement horizontally and a movement vertically which we put together as a ***vector***.

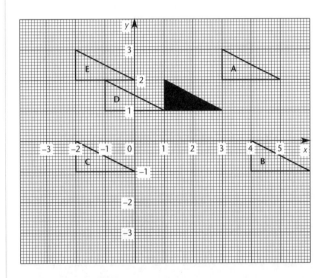

For example, the heavily shaded triangle has been *translated* to position A by moving 2 to the right and 1 up (notice how every point on and in the triangle moves in exactly the same way). We write this movement as a vector $\begin{pmatrix} 2 \\ 1 \end{pmatrix}$

In a similar way we write the following translations:

● To B, 3 to the right and 2 down ... $\begin{pmatrix} 3 \\ -2 \end{pmatrix}$

● To C, 3 to the left and 2 down ... $\begin{pmatrix} -3 \\ -2 \end{pmatrix}$

● To D, 2 to the left, nothing up ... $\begin{pmatrix} -2 \\ 0 \end{pmatrix}$

● To E, 3 to the left and 1 up ... $\begin{pmatrix} -3 \\ 1 \end{pmatrix}$

Notice how we used the *negative* to indicate movement *to the left* and to indicate movement *down*.

TRANSPOSITION

Transposition is the change of a subject in a formula. It is often necessary to change a formula round to help you to find a particular solution to a problem. There is a 'golden rule' of transposition that you need to learn off by heart:

'If it's doing what it's doing to everything else on that side then you can move it to the other side of the equation and make it do the opposite thing.'

Look through the following short examples to see this in action:

● $w = t + 5k$
We could move the t, the $5k$ or the w to give
$$w - t = 5k$$
or $w - 5k = t$
or $0 = t + 5k - w$

● $A = bh$
We could move the b, the h or the A to give
$$^A/_b = h$$
or $^A/_h = b$
or $1 = {^{bh}/_A}$

● $Y = \dfrac{t + 2}{d}$
We could move the $(t + 2)$, the d or the Y to give
$$\frac{Y}{t + 2} = \frac{1}{d}$$
or $Yd = t + 2$
or $1 = \dfrac{t + 2}{Yd}$

> *Remember: Only try to move one term at a time.*

$p = m (x - 3)$
We could move the m, the $(x - 3)$ or the p to give

$\dfrac{p}{m} = x - 3$ or $\dfrac{p}{x - 3} = m$ or $1 = \dfrac{m}{p} (x - 3)$

To fully transpose a formula though, is to make another letter the *subject* of that formula. This is often like sculpturing; in mathematics we need to mould our formula into what we want. This can be done as long as we remember to use our 'golden rule'.
See the following examples of this in action:

● Make x the subject of the formula $y = 4 (3x - 1)$.
We move things round until we finally end up with $x = ...$ hence expand to give
$$y = 12x - 4$$
then $y + 4 = 12x$
and $\dfrac{y + 4}{12} = x$

● Make *t* the subject of the formula $s = \dfrac{7 + t^2}{3}$

We move things round until we finally end up with
t = ...

hence $3s = 7 + t^2$

and $\sqrt{(3s - 7)} = t$

TRANSVERSAL

The diagram shows a pair of straight parallel lines
and another straight line passing through them. This
line passing through the parallel lines is called a
transversal.

The angles created are shown as *a* and *b* and will
be equal; they are called *alternate angles*. Both angles
on the same side of the transversal are called *allied
angles* and as such add up to 180°.

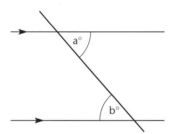

Transversal

TRAPEZIUM

A trapezium is a **quadrilateral** that has a pair of sides
parallel, as shown.

The area of a trapezium is found by multiplying
the height by the average length of the parallel sides.
This is usually written as:

$$\text{area} = \frac{h}{2}(a + b) \quad \text{or} \quad h\frac{(a + b)}{2}$$

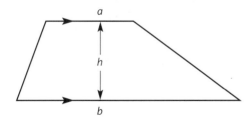

Trapezium

where *a* and *b* are the lengths of the two parallel sides.

TRAPEZOIDAL METHOD (TRAPEZIUM RULE)

(This is a Higher Level topic only.)

The trapezoidal method is a way of approximating
the area under a curve by splitting that area up into

trapeziums and finding the sum of all their areas
added together.

For example, the area below the curve shown has
been split up into a number of trapeziums and it is a
simple matter of calculating the area of each one and
adding them together.

Note how the more trapeziums you split a shape
into, the more accurate becomes your estimated area.
(Find out all about this in A level mathematics!)

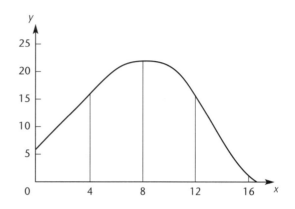

> *Remember: In a velocity/time graph, the arc
> under the curve is the distance covered.*

TRAVEL GRAPHS

Travel graphs are distance/time graphs that represent
a journey. The ones shown illustrate particular
situations. Note how the **gradient** of a line on a
distance/time graph indicates the **speed** of travel.

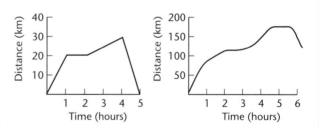

Travel graphs often appear within a GCSE
examination and ought to be read carefully and
accurately. The biggest errors tend to be the
misreading of scales or units on the axes.

Exam Question

On a quiet Sunday morning, a police motorcycle parked
in a layby was passed by a car. The police motor cyclist,
suspecting that the car was exceeding the speed limit,
set off after the car, overtook it and indicated that it
should stop.

The straight line graph represents the car's journey
over the first 30 seconds after passing the motor cycle.

(a) What does the gradient of the straight line graph
represent? The police motor cycle's journey is
indicated in the table overleaf.

Time (seconds)	10	20	30	40	50	60
Distance (metres) from layby	180	460	880	980	1020	1020

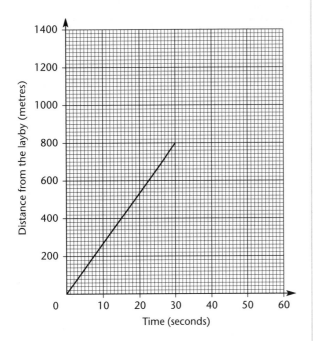

(b) On the same graph, plot the points representing the information in the above table and join them up with a smooth curve to represent the journey of the police motor cycle.

(c) After how many seconds did the police motor cycle draw level with the car?

(d) The car slowed down and stopped 20 metres behind the police motor cycle.

Complete the graph of the car's journey to illustrate the car slowing down and stopping.

(NEAB; I)

Solution

(a) The speed, or 1600 m/minute, or 96 km/hour.

(b) See the second figure.

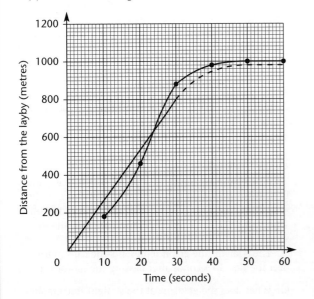

(c) 24 seconds, where the two lines cross.

(d) See the dashed line on the figure above.

TREE DIAGRAMS

A tree diagram is a particular way of illustrating all the events under consideration within a situation, with a view to calculating some probabilities. The diagram looks like branches of a tree and hence the name.

For example, the probability of Philip getting his maths homework correct is 0.4, while the probability of Tim's Dad getting it correct is 0.8. What is the probability of only one of them getting the maths homework correct?

Philip	Tim's Dad		Result	Probability
	0.8	right	Both right	0.4 × 0.8 = 0.32
0.4 right	0.2	wrong	Only Philip right	0.4 × 0.2 = 0.08
	0.8	right	Only Tim's Dad right	0.6 × 0.8 = 0.48
0.6 wrong	0.2	wrong	Both wrong	0.6 × 0.2 = 0.12

> *Remember: The probabilities on each pair of branches will always add up to 1.*

If we draw a tree diagram and complete it by putting the probabilities on the branches it will look as shown. The calculation proceeds as follows:

● We use the AND rule to multiply the probabilities along the branches in order to find the probabilities of each event in the end column.

● But then we need to use the OR rule to calculate the probability of either Philip or Tim's Dad getting the homework correct.

● That is to say, we *add* together the two probabilities, which will give us 0.08 + 0.48, which is 0.56.

If the question had been 'what is the probability of at least one of them getting the maths homework correct', then you would need to add together the probability 0.32 + 0.48 + 0.08 = 0.88.

The error to avoid while using tree diagrams is the obvious one of getting the adding and the multiplication routines mixed up. Or in fact, to use a tree diagram when it is not really helpful. If you know that you only need *one branch* of the tree diagram, then there is no need to draw the whole thing out, just the branch that you need. But do make sure that this really is all you need.

✦ *Combined events, Probability*

TRIAL AND IMPROVEMENT

The method of using trial and improvement to solve equations is one used by computers and is a good way to solve an equation that you cannot do by any other method. It is a method that always strives to get closer and closer to the solution until close enough.

The most likely type of equation you will be asked to solve by trial and improvement at GCSE is a cubic one like the following example.

Example

Solve the equation $x^3 + x = 400$ giving your solution to one decimal place.

Solution

We must first find the two whole numbers that x lies between, and we do this by intelligent guessing.

Try $x = 7$: $343 + 7 = 350$, too small – next trial needs to be higher.

Try $x = 8$: $512 + 8 = 520$, too high.

But we now know the solution is between 7 and 8.

We now have to find two consecutive one decimal place numbers that the solution lies between:

We must now try halfway between 7 and 8 which we see is 7.5

Try 7.5: $421.875 + 7.5 = 429.375$, too high, but we can see that we are close, we can improve the trial by trying 7.3

Try 7.3: $389.017 + 7.3 = 396.317$, too low, but only just, so we can improve the trial by trying 7.4

Try 7.4: $405.224 + 7.4 = 412.624$ too high, but we now know the solution is between 7.3 and 7.4

These are the two consecutive one decimal place numbers that the solution lies between.

To find which is closer we cannot just look at the numbers we have because the differences do not go up uniformly. We have to try halfway between again and go from there. Halfway between 7.3 and 7.4 is 7.35

Try 7.35: $397.06537 + 7.35 = 404.41537$, too high.

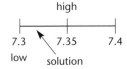

So you see the solution is nearest to 7.3 (to one decimal place)

> Remember: You must search the extra decimal place to justify your final answer – or lose a mark.

If the question had said 'give the solution to two decimal places', then we would have to continue the search and find two consecutive two decimal place numbers and repeat the halfway search.

Exam Question

(a) Show that a solution of the equation $x^3 + x = 15$ lies between 2 and 3.
(b) Use the method of trial and improvement to find this solution of the equation $x^3 + x = 15$. Give your answer to 1 decimal place.

Solution

(a) Substitute $x = 2$, to get $2^3 + 2 = 10$, too small substitute $x = 3$, to get $3^3 + 3 = 30$, too big
(b) Try $x = 2.5$, to get 18.125, too big
$x = 2.3$, to get 14.467, too small
$x = 2.4$, to get 16.224, too big

we now know the solution is between 2.3 and 2.4 try halfway between these, 2.35, to get 15.327875 too big, so the lower number, 2.3 must be closer than 2.4 the solution is $x = 2.3$

TRIANGLES

A triangle is a plane shape with three straight sides. There are a number of special triangles that you ought to be familiar with.

Types of triangle

Isosceles triangle

This has two of its sides the same and two angles the same. It has one *line of symmetry* bisecting the angle included between the two equal sides.

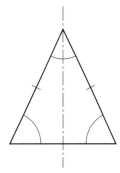

Isosceles triangle

Equilateral triangle

This has all its sides the same length and all its angles are 60°. It has three *lines of symmetry* bisecting each angle, and its order of *rotational symmetry* is three.

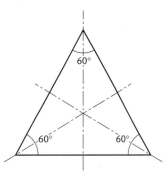

Equilateral triangle

Right-angled triangle

This is one that contains a right angle.

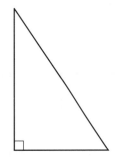

Right-angled triangle

Scalene triangle

This is one which has all three sides a different length.

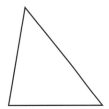

Scalene triangle

Areas of triangles

The *area* of a triangle is calculated by multiplying half its base length by the perpendicular height.

area of triangle = $\frac{1}{2}$ × base length × perpendicular height

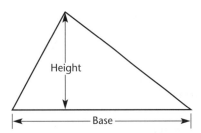

If we know two sides and the included angle of a triangle, then we can calculate the area of a triangle by using trigonometry to calculate the perpendicular height. We then use the previous formula.

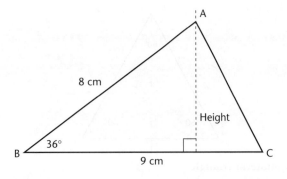

For example, to find the area of triangle ABC, drop a perpendicular line down from A to BC, as shown. Calculate the perpendicular height by trigonometry: height/8 = sin 36°, so height = 8 × sine 36°.

This gives us 4.7 cm, and the area is now calculated by half of 4.7 × 9, which gives us 21.15 cm^2.

Exam Question

A window cleaner uses a ladder 8.5 m long. The ladder leans against the vertical wall of a house with the foot of the ladder 2.0 m from the wall on horizontal ground.

(a) Calculate the size of the angle which the ladder makes with the ground.
(b) Calculate the height of the top of the ladder above the ground.
(c) The window cleaner climbs 6.0 m up the ladder (see diagram). How far is his lower foot from the wall?

(MEG; I)

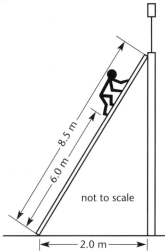

not to scale

Solution

(a) Recognize the cosine situation, and that

$$\cos x = \frac{2}{8.5} = 0.2353$$

hence $x = \cos^{-1} 0.2353 = 76°$

(b) Recognize the Pythagoras situation, and
height^2 = 8.5^2 – 2^2 = 68.25
hence height = $\sqrt{68.25}$ = 8.26 m.

(c) There are various methods including using similar triangles as well as trigonometry. The simplest perhaps is trigonometry and to calculate 2.5 cos 76°, which (using the accurate value of 76°) is 0.59 m.

Congruent triangles

Congruent triangles are triangles that are exactly the same as each other, in angles and in length.

✦ *Congruency*

Similar triangles

Similar triangles are two triangles that are the same shape, that is their angles correspond to each other, but one is smaller than the other by some scale factor. In this case the ratios of corresponding pairs of sides are equal, and are the same as the scale factor of enlargement for the two triangles.

⊹ Similarity

TRIGONOMETRICAL GRAPHS

⊹ Graphs

TRIGONOMETRY

Trigonometry is the study of features of triangles, mainly to do with angles and sides. The usual abbreviation of trigonometry is trig. The most common use of trig is within right-angled triangles, and it is in these that our trig functions are defined:

In any right-angled triangle we call the longest side, which is always opposite to the right angle, the hypotenuse.

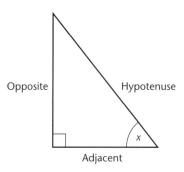

Then, depending on which angle of the triangle we are finding or using, we name the other two sides. The side opposite to the angle is called the opposite; while the side next to both the angle and the right angle is called the adjacent.

Then for any given angle x:

tan x = opposite/adjacent
sin x = opposite/hypotenuse
cos x = adjacent/hypotenuse

> *Remember: Check your calculator is in DEG mode and **NOT** in RAD or GRAD.*

This information is likely to be given on a formula sheet within an examination, but if the facts are known then it makes problem solving much quicker.

One way of remembering the facts is to remember a sentence such as 'Tommy On A Ship Of His Caught All Herring' taking the first letter of each word gives us T = O/A, S = O/H, C = A/H. There are lots of other similar sentences to be made like this to help you to remember the trig fractions. Make up your own!

Note: for the use of tan, sin and cos, see their individual entry in this reference guide.

With this topic there are quite a few mistakes that are made:

● Using the wrong trig function. Do look carefully at which angle you're given or need to find and then work out. Is it tan, sin or cos?

● Often the fraction is written upside down, which will cause problems. So get it the right way up, and notice that sin and cos must be a fraction smaller than 1.

● Candidates often make mistakes because they have not got a clear diagram of the situation. So they either calculate the wrong angle altogether or just use the wrong data. Start with a clear diagram of the problem given, especially if the problem has come from a three-dimensional situation.

Exam Question
A cable car route is in two stages.
Safety experts have decided that a cable car stage is safe only if the angle of elevation is less than 68° and greater than 30°.
(a) Calculate the angles of elevation, x. and y, indicated on the diagram.
    (i) x
    (ii) y
(b) Based on the information given, is each stage shown of this route safe? Give reasons for your answers.

(NEAB; I)

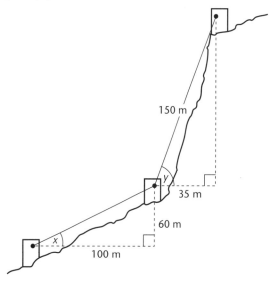

Solution
(a) (i) Recognize the tan situation to give tan x = $\frac{60}{100}$ = 0.6
      hence x = tan^{-1}0.6 = 31°
   (ii) Recognize the cos situation to give cos y = $\frac{35}{150}$ = 0.2333
      hence y = cos^{-1}0.2333 = 76.5° or 77°
(b) The first stage is safe since x = 31° and this is between the acceptable angles. Yet the second stage is not safe since the angle y = 77° greater than the highest safe angle of 68°.

Exam Question

The diagram shows an 8 m ladder leaning against a wall.

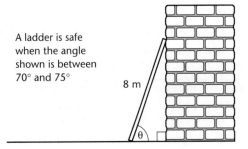

A ladder is safe when the angle shown is between 70° and 75°

Instructions for finding the safest position for the foot of the ladder are also given.

(a) An 8 m ladder is placed against a wall using the safety instructions above. Calculate the furthest away from the wall the foot of the ladder can be.

(b) Calculate the furthest up the wall this ladder will reach when it is in a safe position.

Solution

(a) The furthest distance away from the wall will be when the angle is at its smallest possible, which is at 70°.

This is a cosine situation.

$$\frac{x}{8} = \cos 70$$

$x = 8 \times \cos 70 = 2.74$ metres.

(b) The furthest distance up the wall is when the angle is at its greatest possible, which is at 75°

This is a sine situation

$$\frac{y}{8} = \sin 70$$

$y = 8 \times \sin 70 = 7.52$ metres

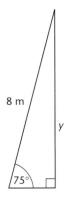

CHECKPOINT

(a) Calculate sin 50° + cos 40° + tan 65°

(b) What angle has a cosine of 0.111?

(c) What angle has a sine of 0.333?

(d) What angle has a tangent of 0.777?

TRUNCATE

This means to cut off, or shorten. In mathematics, it means to remove the decimal fraction.

Units

You need to be aware of the two systems of units that operate within our society. These are the **metric** and the **imperial** systems.

The metric system

Examples of metric system units are:

1 kilogram = 1,000 grams
1 kilometre = 1,000 metres
1 kilowatt = 1,000 watts

> Remember: The word 'kilo' means 1,000 the word 'milli' means $\frac{1}{1,000}$ th.

1,000 kilograms   = 1 tonne
10 millimetres   = 1 centimetre
100 centimetres   = 1 metre
1,000 millimetres = 1 metre
1,000 millilitres = 1 litre

These ought to be learnt.

The imperial system

Examples of Imperial system units are:

12 inches = 1 foot
3 feet   = 1 yard
16 ounces = 1 pound
8 pints   = 1 gallon

There are plenty more Imperial units. However, these are the more common ones that you would be expected to be familiar with, although you would not be expected to learn them.

Equivalence of units

You ought to be aware of the approximate conversion from the popular *Imperial units* to the *metric*:

2 pounds weight is approximately 1 kilogram
3 feet is approximately 1 metre
5 miles is approximately 8 kilometres
1 gallon is approximately 4.5 litres

Although you will find conversion questions in some GCSE examination papers, the conversion factor is often given. The biggest error associated with units is the *lack* of them in an answer or the use of the *wrong ones*.

When a question is asked, then the answer (if it has units like cm, kg, m.p.h., etc) should be given in the *correct* units. You could lose marks if no units are given or the wrong ones are used. So always *check* that the units you have used are indeed the ones used in the question, unless you have needed to convert them to a more appropriate unit.

For example, what is the length of a street that is equivalent to 150 paving slabs end-to-end, where the slabs are each 75 cm long?

We simply multiply 75 cm by 150. This comes to 11,250 cm. Yet it would be more sensible to give the answer as 112.5 metres.

VARIABLE

A variable is something that can change. People's moods are variable, since they can change from day to day and even minute to minute.

In mathematics a variable is usually a letter in an algebraic expression that stands for something that can change. For example, the formula for the area of a rectangle is area = length × base, i.e. $A = l \times b$ where A, l and b are all variables as they can all be different values depending on the particular rectangle.

Variables are commonly used in computer programs in just the same way. For example, you can define a *loop* or an expression with a variable:

FOR I = 1 TO 15

This is the start of a computer program loop where the I will vary from 1 to 15 as the program loops round.

VARIATION

Variation is the study of how one thing is in proportion to another.

-+- *Proportion*

VAT

VAT is the word that means 'Value Added Tax'. It is a tax that the government places on goods in order to help raise revenue from its people. It is a percentage rate; at the moment this rate is 17.5% on most goods, but there are a few categories where this rate is zero, for example children's clothes and books.

For example, if a television is sold at a price of £481.75, including the 17.5% VAT, how much money will go to the government as VAT?

The final price included the 17.5% VAT and therefore represented 117.5% of the pre-tax price. Hence the pre-tax price was 481.75 × 100/117.5 which is £410, so the VAT is the difference of £71.75

-+- *Taxes*

VECTORS

The scientists will properly define a vector as a force having direction and magnitude, yet the use we put it to in GCSE Mathematics is not always as rigid as that.

In mathematics a vector can be thought of as a displacement, a movement from one place to another. This displacement is defined by its horizontal and vertical movement.

Vector notation

There are three common ways to write a vector:

- Write it as $\overrightarrow{AB}$ where AB is some given line and the direction of the vector is from A to B.

- Label it as $\underline{a}$ or a to denote that this is a vector; there could well be an arrow on the line to show the direction of the vector.

- It can simply be defined as the column vector $\binom{a}{b}$ where a is the movement horizontally to the right (so a negative value will indicate movement to the left), and b is the vertical movement up (so a negative value will indicate a movement down). See the examples shown.

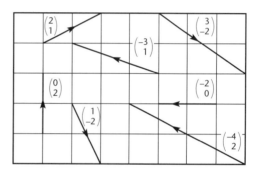

Vector addition

We *add* vectors together as the sum of their movements. Notice how the sum of the two vectors $\underline{a}$ and $\underline{b}$ is represented by one vector $\underline{a} + \underline{b}$ that is by the sum of its horizontal movements and of its vertical movements.

In other words: $\binom{3}{1} + \binom{4}{-3} = \binom{7}{-2}$

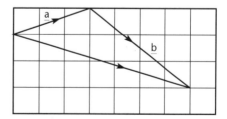

Vector subtraction

We *subtract* two vectors by adding the *negative* of the vector to be subtracted.

So the previous example becomes $\binom{3}{1} + \binom{-4}{3}$. As we can see from the diagram on the next page, the subtraction of the two vectors used in the addition $\underline{a} + \underline{b}$ can be seen as the subtraction of their movements.

In other words: $\begin{pmatrix} 3 \\ 1 \end{pmatrix} - \begin{pmatrix} 4 \\ -3 \end{pmatrix} = \begin{pmatrix} -1 \\ 4 \end{pmatrix}$

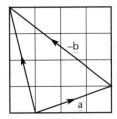

Vector multiplication

We *multiply* vectors by repeated addition. That is to say $3\underline{a} = \underline{a} + \underline{a} + \underline{a}$ as shown. Also $\frac{1}{2}\underline{a}$ will be half the vector $\underline{a}$ as also seen on the figure.

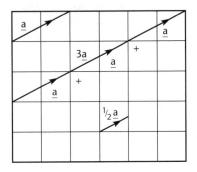

Position vectors

The position vector of a point is the column vector from a defined origin to that point. For example the position vector of the point D shown is $\begin{pmatrix} 3 \\ 4 \end{pmatrix}$

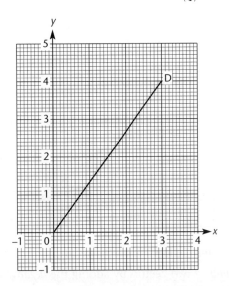

Note the similarity between the position vector and the co-ordinate of D. However, also note the difference, since a common mistake is to write down the co-ordinate instead of the position vector.

Parallel vectors

If two vectors have the same column vector or are defined as being equal, then they are both parallel and of the same magnitude.

If one vector is a multiple of another, then those two vectors are parallel to each other. For example, the vectors $\underline{a}$ and $4\underline{a}$ are parallel to each other and $4\underline{a}$ is four times as long (or as big) as $\underline{a}$.

Exam Question
In the triangle shown,

$$\vec{AB} = \mathbf{p} \text{ and } \vec{AC} = \mathbf{q}$$

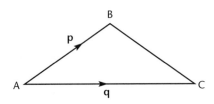

(a) Express $\vec{BC}$ in terms of $\mathbf{p}$ and $\mathbf{q}$
(b) Given that M and N are the mid-points of *AB* and *AC* respectively, express in terms of $\mathbf{p}$ and $\mathbf{q}$
   (i) $\vec{MB}$,
   (ii) $\vec{MN}$.
(c) What *two* facts can you deduce about the line *MN* from the result obtained in (b) part (ii)?

(NEAB; H)

Solution
(a) $\vec{BC} = \mathbf{q} - \mathbf{p}$
(b) (i) $\vec{MB} = \frac{1}{2}\mathbf{p}$ (ii) $\vec{MN} = \frac{1}{2}\mathbf{q} - \frac{1}{2}\mathbf{p} = \frac{1}{2}(\mathbf{q} - \mathbf{p})$
(c) MN is parallel to BC and,
   MN is half the length of BC.

VERTEX

A vertex is a point where two lines or two edges meet. The plural of vertex is *vertices*. The vertices of plane shapes are the sharp corners where the angles are found. The vertex of a pyramid is the top where all the edges meet.

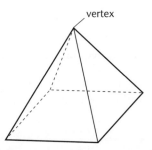

Vertex

Exam Questions
The net for a solid is shown on the next page. On the diagram mark with an X the other point or points that will meet the point A to form a vertex when the solid is made.

(NEAB; I)

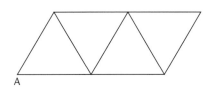

A

Solution

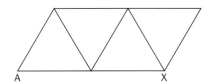

A   X

VIEWS

When looking at solid shapes you get different views depending on which direction you look at the shape. The two important views are the plans and the elevations.

Plans

The plan of a shape is the view you get when you look directly overhead down onto the shape. An example is shown.

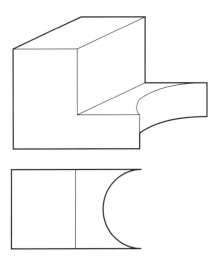

View; plan

Elevation

There are two types of elevation, *end elevation* and *front elevation*. The end elevation is the view you get of the shape when you view it from the end; the front elevation is the view seen from the front. An example is shown.

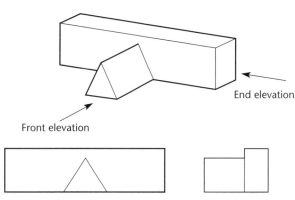

End elevation

Front elevation

View; elevations

The most common error made with views is to try and make them look three-dimensional instead of *two-dimensional*. You must not try to put any *perspective* into the diagram; nor should you draw what you *think* you would see (because we see in three dimensions, and not in two dimensions). Draw the shape of the top, or the end, or the front!

VOLUME

Volume is the space occupied by a solid, three-dimensional shape. It is measured in cubes, that is cubic metres or m³, etc.

You ought to be familiar with the following formulae for finding volumes:

- Cuboid = length × breadth × height.

- Prism = regular cross section × length.

- Sphere = $\frac{4}{3}\pi r^3$

- Pyramid = $\frac{1}{3}$ × base area × vertical height.

> *Remember: Do be familiar with which formula you are given in the exam and which you must learn.*

The most common error here is to use the wrong formula. It is helpful to you to learn these formulae, but if you can't, then you will find them on the formula sheet given to you in the examination.

VULGAR FRACTION

This is a fraction in which both numerator and denominator are whole numbers, e.g. $\frac{3}{4}$.

WAGES

Wages are the payments made to employees by the employers. That is to say, the pay given to the workers by those who hired them. Wages are usually defined as weekly payments and can often vary with the number of hours worked or the number of articles made or jobs done.

If someone has a basic working week of 40 hours, then any hours extra to this time is called overtime. Overtime is usually paid by various rates:

- time and a quarter is basic hourly rate × 1.25
- time and a half   is basic hourly rate × 1.5
- double time   is basic hourly rate × 2

For example, John worked a 43-hour week, where his basic week is 38 hours at a rate of £4.50 per hour. His overtime rate is time and a quarter. What is his week's wage?

The basic pay is £4.50 × 38 = £171
The overtime pay is £4.50 × (43 − 38) × 1.25 = £28.12
Hence the total pay is £199.12

Of course tax would probably have to be paid on this wage but the question has not asked us to calculate that here.

Exam Question
Maria earns £3.90 for each hour she works as a shop assistant. She works from 9 a.m. to 1 p.m. and from 2 p.m. to 6 p.m. each day for five days a week.

(a) Calculate Maria's weekly wage.
(b) Maria is asked to work four hours' overtime on her day off. She is paid twice the rate of £3.90 per hour. What is Maria paid for working the four hours' overtime?

(NEAB; F)

Solution
(a) 8 hours each day. Hence weekly wage will be 8 × 5 × £3.90 = £156
(b) Overtime rate = £3.90 × 2 = £7.80.
    Hence overtime pay = £7.80 × 4 = £31.20.

WEIGHING SCALES

Weighing scales come in all sorts of shapes and sizes, yet in most cases the scale we have to read is similar to the ones shown. You must be able to read quite accurately the readings on weighing scales, as well as on the other types of scales you will come across.

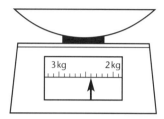

In the first weighing scale, notice how the scale reads from right to left. Between each kilogram the space is divided into ten parts, and as one tenth of 1 kg is 100 grams, each small line represents 100 g. You can see that the pointer is on the fourth line between the 2 kg and 3 kg marks so the object we are weighing is 2 kg 400 g, or 2.4 kg.

Notice how on the second weighing scale the space between each kilogram is divided into five parts, each line representing one-fifth of a kilogram, which is 200 grams. Hence the pointer is pointing to 3 kg 600 g or 3.6 kg.

Now look at the third weighing scale. The space between the kilogram is divided into ten large parts (longer lines), each one now representing 100 g (or 0.10 kg), and each of these spaces is divided into two parts, each one 50 g (0.05 kg). The pointer on the diagram is pointing to 0.25 kg.

CHECKPOINT ANSWERS

Accuracy
(i) 50
(ii) 45
(iii) 45.2

And rule $\frac{1}{6} \times \frac{1}{6} \times \frac{1}{6} = 1/216$

Average
(i) mode = 2
(ii) median = 5
(iii) mean = 48 ÷ 11 = 4.36 (rounded)

Bearings 138° + 180° = 318°

Circle
(i) circumference = $2\pi r$
(ii) area = πr^2

Common factors and multiples
(i) HCF = 8
(ii) LCM = 105

Constructions (i)

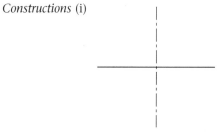

(ii)

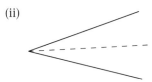

(iii)

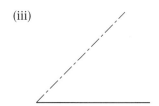

Cosine
(i) 0.906
(ii) 48.2°
(iii) 2.9 cm (rounded)

Cumulative frequency
(i) Calculate the difference between the upper and the lower quartile.
(ii) 50%

Density Use the capital letters shown to make the triangle

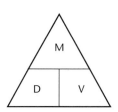

This is used to show
mass = density × volume

$$\text{density} = \frac{\text{mass}}{\text{volume}}$$

$$\text{volume} = \frac{\text{mass}}{\text{density}}$$

Equations
(i) $x = 1.4$
(ii) $x = -2$ and $x = 3$
(iii) $x = 2$ and $y = 1$

Frequency
(i) Create another column of 'midway × frequency' then sum this column and divide by the total frequency.

Score x	Frequency	midway × frequency
$0 < x \leqslant 20$	3	10 × 3 = 30
$20 < x \leqslant 40$	9	30 × 9 = 270
$40 < x \leqslant 60$	23	50 × 23 = 1,150
$60 < x \leqslant 80$	11	70 × 11 = 770
$80 < x \leqslant 100$	4	90 × 4 = 360
Total	50	2,580

The estimated mean = 2580 ÷ 50 = 51.6 marks

(ii) construct a cumulative frequency column, plot and draw a cumulative frequency diagram and read off the estimated median.

Score x	Frequency	Cumulative frequency (less than)
$0 < x \leqslant 20$	3	3
$20 < x \leqslant 40$	9	12
$40 < x \leqslant 60$	23	35
$60 < x \leqslant 80$	11	46
$80 < x \leqslant 100$	4	50

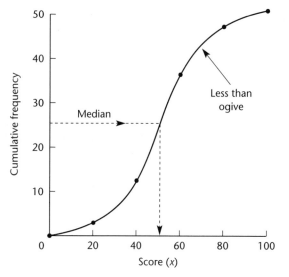

The estimated median is read as 52 marks

Generalize	(i) $7n - 3$
	(ii) $n^2 + 3$
Hexagon	(i) 6
	(ii) 6
	(iii) $360° \div 6 = 60°$
	(iv) $180° - 60 = 120°$
Index	(i) 6×10^6
	(ii) 7.5×10^{-3}
Irrational	the irrational numbers are $\sqrt{3}$, $(\pi - 3)$, 5π
Lines of Symmetry	18
Metric	(i) $10 \times 10 = 100$
	(ii) $100 \times 100 = 10,000$
	(iii) $100 \times 100 \times 100 = 1,000,000$

Nets

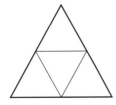

This is not the only net you could have drawn, but it's the most common one shown to be the net of a tetrahedron.

Or rule	$4/52 + 4/52 = 8/52 = 2/13$ (or 0.154)
Percentage	(i) £115 × 5 ÷ 100 = £5.75
	(ii) 450 g × 0.92 = 414 g
	(iii) 5.40 ÷ 80 × 100 = 6.75%
Polygon	(i) $360 \div 8 = 45°$
	(ii) $180 - (360 \div 10) = 144°$
Prime	23, 29, 31, 37, 41, 43, 47
Probability	(i) $4/52 \times 4/51 = 16/2652 = 0.006$
	(ii) 2 × part(i) = 32/2652 = 0.012
Pythagoras	(i) If the two given sides are both the 'small sides', then hypotenuse = $\sqrt{(5^2 + 4^2)} = 6.4$ cm
	(ii) If the 5 cm is the hypotenuse, then small side = $\sqrt{(5^2 - 4^2)} = 3$ cm

(You may have recognized this last case as the 3, 4, 5 triangle and gone straight to the answer. Well done.)

Quadratic	(i) $6x^2 - 8x + 15x - 20$
	$6x^2 + 7x - 20$
	(ii) $(x + 5)(x - 2)$
Ratio	(i) 9 : 16
	(ii) 27 : 64
Rational	There are lots of correct answers, some of the simplest to see are $(\pi + 1)$ or $\sqrt{20}$
Rounding	(i) 3,200
	(ii) 3,199
	(iii) 3,198.6
Simultaneous equations	$x = 5$, $y = 7$
Sine	(i) 0.643 (rounded)
	(ii) 27.1° (rounded)

Speed   Use the capital letters shown to make the triangle

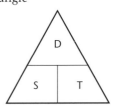

This is used to show
distance = speed × time

$$speed = \frac{distance}{time}$$

$$time = \frac{distance}{speed}$$

Standard form	(i) 5×10^6
	(ii) 1×10^{-6}
Symmetry	(i) Nine lines of symmetry and rotational symmetry of order nine.
	(ii) No lines of symmetry and rotational symmetry of order two.
Tangent	(i) 5.67 (rounded)
	(ii) 26.6° (rounded)
	(iii) 56.3° (rounded)
Trigonometry	(i) 3.6765958
	(ii) 83.6° (rounded)
	(iii) 19.5° (rounded)
	(iv) 37.8° (rounded)